Acknowledgei

I should like to express my gratitu
individuals and organisations for providing help and information and for allowing me to quote freely from letters, memoirs, diaries and books: the Air Historical Branch (RAF), the late Squadron Leader Dennis Armitage and Mrs Margaret Armitage, Maurice Bann, Tony Chadwick, Cheshire Archives and Local Studies (for quotations from the *Macclesfield Courier* and *Macclesfield Times)*, Margaret Mason-Cox of the Hutchins School, Tasmania, Anselm Cramer OSB, Archivist, Ampleforth Abbey, the late Wing Commander Bob Doe, Sue Edge, Flight Lieutenant John Greenwood, Wing Commander Guy Harris, Mark Harris (Supermarine Aero Engineering Ltd), Joan Harrison, Hull History Centre, the Imperial War Museum, the *London Gazette*, Macclesfield Historical Aviation Society, Macclesfield Library, the late Air Vice-Marshal 'Johnnie' Johnson, Dr Emily Mayhew, the late Dr Gordon Mitchell, Geoffrey Moore (Stoke-on-Trent Association of Engineers), the National Archives, RAF ACOS (Manning), the RAF Museum, Hendon, John Shipman, Stoke-on-Trent City Archives, the staff of the Learning Resource Centre at Stoke-on-Trent College, the staff of Trentham Library (especially Catherine Walters and Neil Fox) and the late Wing Commander 'Jas' Storrar. I am especially grateful to Nic Morton for sharing his research into the life of his great uncle Leslie Pidd. I should also like to express a general debt to all the sources listed in the bibliography.

Acknowledgement is also made for permission to include extracts from the following: *Enemy Coast Ahead* by Guy Gibson, reprinted by permission of Crecy Publishing; *The Last Enemy* by Richard Hillary (copyright

© Richard Hillary, 1942), reprinted by permission of A. M. Heath & Co. Ltd; *Five of the Few* by Steve Darlow, published by Grub Street; *The Kent College Saga* by Margaret James, reprinted by permission of the Headmistress of Kent College; and *Under the Wire* by William Ash, published by Bantam Books, reprinted by permission of The Random House Group Ltd. An extract from Ronald Wallens' *Flying made my Arms Ache* is used courtesy of Mrs Vicky Wallens and extracts from Gordon Batt's war memoir are reproduced by permission of Bill Bond and the Battle of Britain Historical Society.

Photographs and other illustrations were provided by Sylvia and Peter Baddeley, Maurice Bann, Nick de Carteret (nephew of Harold Fenton), Eileen Hallam, Malcolm Mann, Edward McManus and the Battle of Britain London Monument, R. B. Marchant and the Guinea Pig Club, RAF Manston Spitfire & Hurricane Trust, the RAF Museum, the late Jules Pidd, Wilhelm Ratuszynski, the *Shropshire Magazine,* Staffordshire Sentinel News & Media Ltd., Angela Urwin-Mann and acesofww2.com, Squadron Leader Brian Waite, John Walch, Vicky Wallens, The War Graves Photographic Project and Shirley Wilson (daughter of George Bennions). Acknowledgement is also made for the use of the Cuthbert Orde portraits (private copyright).

Every effort has been made to trace copyright holders and the author and the Imperial War Museum would be grateful for any information which might help trace those whose identities or addresses are not currently known.

SCRAMBLING TO GLORY

Fighter Pilots of Central England in the Battle of Britain

By

WILLIAM COOKE

Copyright William Cooke

North Staffordshire Press
Newcastle-under-Lyme
Staffordshire

Scrambling to Glory

Fighter Pilots of Central England in the Battle of Britain

ISBN 978-0-9928305-6-4

Published in 2015

By
North Staffordshire Press
Brampton Business Centre
10 Queen Street
The Brampton
Newcastle-under-Lyme
Staffordshire
ST5 1ED

Contents

PART ONE

A FEW OF 'THE FEW'

1
The French Debacle
(10 May–22 June 1940)

For the Belgian dispatch rider standing on the Dunkirk beaches with thousands of other Allied soldiers the sight of a lone Spitfire, high above, taking on four Junkers became symbolic. If the Spitfire came out on top, then they would be rescued. He prayed silently as he watched. The Spitfire shot down two of them, crippled a third, and the fourth fled.

The 'phoney war' was over and the *Blitzkrieg* – lightning war – was living up to its name in the West. Belgium and Holland had surrendered; within weeks Norway and France would follow suit. For the troops on the beaches, bombed and strafed by wave after wave of German planes, salvation lay with the Royal Navy, conspicuously present, and the RAF, largely unseen in the skies above them.

For the inexperienced pilots of Fighter Command, the Battle of France – the overture to the Battle of Britain – was to be a steep learning curve. One of them, on his first sortie over Dunkirk, came up on the radio telephone and asked, 'What are all those black puffs?' 'That's flak, you bloody fool!' came the reply.

In contrast to their battle-hardened *Luftwaffe* counterparts, most of the British pilots had never been in combat. John Ashton had been born at Newcastle-under-Lyme in 1914 and educated at Newcastle High School. Like many of his contemporaries he became fascinated with flying after visiting an air display in his teens, and from then on he saved his pocket money to pay for flying lessons. In February 1939, he joined the RAF Volunteer

Reserve (RAFVR) and received his initial training at Meir Aerodrome in Stoke-on-Trent, followed by a spell at Ternhill, near Market Drayton.

John Ashton

A year later, as a Pilot Officer, he was in France with 85 Squadron as part of the Air Component of the British Expeditionary Force (BEF). He was acutely aware of how much he and his fledgling colleagues had to learn, especially the advantages of flying in the looser units favoured by their opponents rather than in the rigid air-display formations that they had practised so assiduously until then:

> Fighter tactics were picked up from the Germans who had a lot of experience from the Civil War in Spain, such as flying in pairs, or flying in two pairs, the 'finger fours' formation of the four finger-tips.[1]

He also vividly recalled the turmoil of the dogfight:

4

> One moment there is nothing about, then the sky is
> full of aircraft. All you can do is to keep on turning,
> turning, turning, and then you see an aircraft that is
> not one of your own, and it gets into your sights.
> You fire your guns and don't dally because if you
> do somebody else is going to be on your tail.[2]

On 10 May 1940, the first day of the German attack, he shot down two Heinkel 111s and claimed two other 'kills' on the 13th, during a period of intense fighting. On the 15th he had to crash-land in Belgium but was back in action within twenty-four hours. So rapid was the German advance that his squadron was forced to leave their airfield at Lille and withdraw to Merville on the 19 May and then to Boulogne on the following day. Shortly afterwards it returned to Northolt with only four serviceable aircraft, having suffered the worst losses of any squadron based in France.

What was left of the unit was sent to reform at Debden, but some pilots were transferred to other squadrons straightaway. Ashton was posted to 56 Squadron and saw further action when it was attached to 145 Squadron based at Tangmere, which was involved in 'sweeps' over France in an attempt to cover the BEF's retreat to Dunkirk. So desperate was the situation that Ashton was flying five sorties a day. On 27 May, he was with six other fighters when they were set upon by more than fifty single and twin-engine Messerschmitts. Only two of the seven escaped; Ashton was not one of them.

With his Hurricane on fire and half-blinded by engine oil and glycol, he again made a forced landing, managing to get out just before the plane was engulfed in flames. After some time he linked up with a British Army unit on its way to the beaches. 'I never thought I should become a footslogger,' he recalled a few days later, 'but I was glad to join this party, and a splendid lot of fellows I found them. I take my hat off to the BEF for their cheeriness and courage.' When they reached the coast, their ordeal was far from over, however:

> We managed to get dug in in the sand dunes and though the enemy were continually bombing and shelling the beach, there were very few casualties. At length the time came to get to the boats. We waded into the water and on to a pontoon, and then embarked on a fishing drifter. Our journey home took about twelve hours.[3]

He was given a brief leave and returned to the family home in Keele Road, Newcastle, to find that he had been reported 'missing in action', much to the astonishment of his parents who believed that he had a desk job. Within a week he was back with his unit, but his sight had been affected in the fire and he was hospitalised, thereby missing most of the forthcoming battle.

Initially, David Blomeley's war followed a similar pattern. He had been born at Stafford and educated at the King Edward VI Grammar School, after which in December 1937 he joined the RAF on a short service commission. After completing his training, he was posted to 151 Squadron and then seconded to 607 which had suffered considerable losses in the early weeks of the Battle of France. On 14 May 1940, he flew his Hurricane to the French airfield at Vitry and from then on he was almost continuously in action, striving to protect the BEF and also defend the airfield from sustained German attacks. After a hectic week the squadron was ordered home. When Blomeley and three other pilots landed at Croydon their

Hurricanes were so clapped out and full of bullet holes that they were scrapped.

He returned to 151 Squadron and on 29 May destroyed a Messerschmitt 110 over Dunkirk. However, on 8 June, while on escort duty, he had to bale out after his Hurricane was hit by ack-ack fire. Narrowly escaping injury from trigger-happy French soldiers and then capture by the Germans, he managed to find his way to Cherbourg where he was evacuated alongside the troops he had fought so tenaciously to defend.

Two other Staffordshire men were members of 605 Squadron, which had also been thrown into action. Gerry Edge was born at Codsall, and while working at the family metal business in Wolverhampton he had been commissioned as an Auxiliary Air Force Pilot Officer in 1936. At twenty-seven he was older than most and proved to be a daring and skilful pilot, claiming ten 'kills' during May alone. By contrast Mike Cooper-Slipper was still a teenager. He was born at Kinver and had entered the RAF on a short-service commission straight from school in 1938. On his first sortie on 22 May he shot down an He 111, but the following day as he patrolled over Dunkirk he was himself shot up and returned with more than fifty bullet holes in his Hurricane. Before the squadron was pulled from the battle after six days of intensive action, he had added a Stuka dive-bomber and a Junkers 88 to his score.

Michael Crossley's war began in similar vein. Born at Halford in Warwickshire in 1912, he had studied at the College of Aeronautical Engineering before joining the RAF in 1935. By May 1940 he was a Flight Commander with 32 Squadron and must have found it difficult squashing his 6 foot 2 inch frame into the Hurricane's cockpit. His flight flew from Biggin Hill to France on a daily basis; initially, and much to his relief, it never saw the enemy, as is related in his quirky entry in the squadron diary:

> What a shock! Whole outfit up at 3.15 a.m. Going to France. Everyone amazed. Set off to France, land at Abbeville, refuel, hear dreadful stories, get very frightened, do a patrol, see nothing, feel better; do another, see nothing, feel much better; return home, feel grand.

Gerry Edge

His relief was short-lived and from 18 May he too saw constant action, claiming his first two victories – Messerschmitt 109s – on the 19th. By the end of June he had made seven 'kills' and received the Distinguished Flying Cross (DFC) from the King at an investiture at Biggin Hill.

Mike Crossley had been to Eton. Byron ('Ron') Duckenfield started life as a milkman before joining the RAF and training at the flying school at Ternhill. A series of postings followed to several fighter squadrons, and he flew in turn Gauntlets, Hurricanes and then Spitfires as a Sergeant Pilot. However, soon after the outbreak of hostilities, his war almost came to an abrupt end when, on 11 May 1940, he was a passenger on board a Bristol Bombay transport plane that stalled as it came in to land at Bétheniville in France. It crashed, killing the crew and three members of 501 Squadron and injuring most of the others.

As he recovered in a hospital bed in Roehampton, Duckenfield could not in his wildest dreams have imagined what else the future held for him: that he would score four combat victories in the forthcoming Battle of Britain and be awarded the Air Force Cross; that he would be given command of 615 Squadron and take it to the Far East; and that after having to force-land in Burma he would survive two-and-a-half years as a prisoner of the Japanese in the hell-hole of Rangoon jail.

A second member of 501 Squadron was Ken 'Hawkeye' Lee, who had been born in Birmingham in 1915. Another former pupil of the King Edward VI Grammar School, he started work in a paint factory and in 1937 joined the RAFVR, completing his elementary training at Perth in Scotland and then flying at weekends at Ansty, a grass airfield to the east of Coventry. In January 1939, at the request of the RAF, his employer released him for six months' intensive training with the regular service. The 'six months' were to last six years and he would never return to his former job.

He joined 111 Squadron at Northolt which flew Hurricanes, an aircraft with which he was unfamiliar. 'The first morning,' he recalled, 'they took me out and said, "Here's a Hurricane. Go and fly it." It was very different from anything I had flown but I got round and back.'[4] Two months later he was commissioned:

> One day the station warrant officer called me over and said, 'Lee. What are your initials, my boy?' 'K.N.T., sir.' He said, 'Congratulations. You're an officer. Now bugger off and have your lunch in the officers' mess.' I arrived a sergeant pilot and then this day, to my astonishment, I became an officer.[5]

In September he was posted to 501 Squadron and in May 1940 he too left for France and saw Duckenfield's accompanying aircraft dive into the ground. Suddenly the grim reality of war hit home.

While Duckenfield recovered in hospital, Lee made his presence felt, destroying a Do 17 on 12 May, an Me 110 on the 13th, an He 111 on the 27th and another Do 17 on 6 June. Four days later, while attacking a gaggle of Heinkels, his Hurricane was hit and became uncontrollable. There was nothing for it but to bale out, though the only instruction he had ever received for this eventuality was 'to jump and pull the rip cord'. As he was leaving, the tailplane struck his leg and then, while he was descending, French troops opened fire on him. He was eventually evacuated in a little boat and taken to Torquay. A bullet wound to his right hand meant that he was out of action until the 13 July.

Derbyshire's foremost fighter ace, Arthur 'Darky' Clowes, had fought over France with No.1 Squadron since the beginning of the war and had been lucky to escape with his life in an early tussle not with the enemy but with a

French pilot. On 23 November 1939, the French plane collided with his Hurricane and chopped off much of his tail unit. The French pilot had to bale out, but Clowes just managed to get back to base though his Hurricane ended up on its nose. During this frenzied period he won the Distinguished Flying Medal (DFM) and was mentioned in despatches. The citation for his later award of the DFC gave this account of his exploits:

> Sgt Clowes has displayed courage and determination in many combats against the enemy. He has destroyed at least six enemy aircraft. On 14 June 1940, he led his section in combat against five Messerschmitt 109s and destroyed one. He then observed, above him, three further enemy aircraft and, before they could attack his flight, he engaged them. He succeeded in damaging one and in causing the other two to disperse into the clouds. He has displayed great skill and power of leadership.

He went on to add to this score during the Battle of Britain when he was commissioned and given command of a squadron. He survived the war and remained in the RAF, but his promising career was tragically cut short when he died of cancer of the liver in December 1949, aged only thirty-seven.

With Fighter Command's losses mounting alarmingly, its Commander in Chief resisted the pleas of the French and the pressure of Churchill to send more squadrons to France. It was the right decision. By the time of the French surrender, the RAF had lost 959 aircraft, 509 of these being fighters. Losses of the Fairey Battle, an underpowered fighter bomber, were catastrophic, with 137 being lost. The RAFVR was to have flown this plane, and when one of its members saw a Battle returning from France he went over and asked the pilot, 'What are they like?' 'Absolutely bloody useless,' came the reply. 'The Me 110s and 109s slaughtered us.' This made the green recruit even more appreciative of the Hurricane and Spitfire with which he was then familiarising himself.

One of those returning Fairey Battle pilots was James Archibald Findlay MacLachlan, who had been born at Styal in Cheshire. He yearned for something faster and volunteered for Fighter Command, taking part in the Battle of Britain and the later defence of Malta during which his left forearm had to be amputated after he was wounded. Undeterred, he had an artificial limb designed and continued to fly, becoming one of the notable aces of the war. Once he flew a sortie near to Paris accompanied only by F/Lt Geoffrey Page, who had been stationed at RAF Meir in 1940. Page had also become one of the Few and had suffered terrible burns to his hands when he was shot down. In an astonishing ten minutes the two men destroyed six enemy aircraft, a remarkable feat considering they had only one good hand between them. The following month, on a second such sortie, MacLachlan's luck ran out. His Mustang was shot down by flak and he was again seriously wounded. He died in a German field hospital two days later.

The exodus from Dunkirk went on, from late May to early June. Churchill had hoped to save 50,000 men – 100,000, he told his Cabinet, would be 'magnificent'. However, more than 338,000 Allied servicemen were finally snatched from annihilation or captivity, but the cost had been grievously high in men, ships and planes. Fighter Command in particular had taken a hammering. Home defence was reduced to 331 Spitfires and Hurricanes, supported by 150 'second-line' fighters. Only 66 of the 261 Hurricanes dispatched to France had returned.[6] Many pilots had been lost, among them Spitfire pilot Sgt Leslie James White, of May Bank, Newcastle-under-Lyme, who was killed in action on 1 June 1940 flying with 222 Squadron. He was twenty-three.

James MacLachlan with his personal insignia on the nose panel of his Hurricane.

Squadrons, anxious for replacements, were joined by young lads, many of whom were in their teens and who still delighted in schoolboys' nicknames – 'Razz', 'Cocky', 'Lulu', 'Sneezy', 'Dopey', – while 'older' pilots of twenty-four upwards were invariably 'Uncle' or 'Daddy'. Even some 'aces' (five kills) were astonishingly young. In the fighting over France, one pilot had claimed his five victories in a week, been shot down and awarded the DFC – all at nineteen. On his return to England his mother greeted him with the words: 'I hope you haven't got into any bad habits in France at your age.'[7]

According to the celebrated ace Eric Lock, a fighter pilot could not be considered experienced until he had been shot down and baled out three times, landed in the sea three times, and force-landed three times. By his standards, by any standards, the replacement pilots were 'raw' indeed. When Tony Pickering, from Foxton, Leicestershire, arrived at 32 Squadron the commander asked him the standard question: 'How many hours have you done on Hurricanes?' Pickering replied: 'I have never seen one before, sir.'

A useful source of supply would have been the number of trained fighter pilots who had escaped from Europe, but communication problems were holding them back. Some struggled not only with RAF colloquialisms such as *'prang'* (crash) or *'bought it'* (killed), but also with operational language. *'Tally-ho!'* – the huntsman's cry used by a fighter pilot on sighting enemy aircraft – might have been appropriate for John Peel, the commander of 145 Squadron but was not so meaningful for Sgt Plzak of 310 (Czech) Squadron. One (probably apocryphal) story that did the rounds concerned the clock code that was used to indicate the location of enemy aircraft. A British commander took a foreign pilot to task and wanted to know why he had returned to base immediately after being told that there were 'bandits at three o'clock'. 'Because it's only half past one,' came the reply.[8]

On 18 June, in a speech to the Commons, Churchill warned the nation of the ordeal to come:

> The Battle of France is over. I expect that the Battle of Britain is about to begin. Upon this battle depends the survival of Christian civilisation... Hitler knows he will have to break us in this island or lose the war.[9]

A few days later, on 22 June, Hitler humiliated the French by insisting that they sign the armistice in the same train carriage in which Germany had surrendered in 1918. In a few months he had accomplished what the German High Command had signally failed to do in four years in the First War.

Unsurprisingly, he was at his most confident. 'The English have lost the war, but they haven't yet noticed it,' he declared,[10] a view that was shared by most of the world. He half expected Britain to remove Churchill – who had been Prime Minister for only a few weeks – and come to terms. At this stage his attitude toward invasion was ambivalent. Although the British Army had been defeated and the RAF given a mauling, they had not been destroyed, and the Royal Navy was far superior to the *Kriegsmarine*, the German navy. Any such enterprise would at best have been perilous, at worst suicidal. Initially therefore Hitler showed scant interest in invading, and while Churchill was galvanising and unifying the nation as never before, he went sightseeing in Paris. In Britain there was a strange sense of relief that at last they stood alone. A popular slogan of the day was 'We're in the Final – and we're playing at Home'.

By the end of June, when it was obvious that Britain remained resolute, Hitler decided that a massive show of air power would bring his opponents into line. He turned to Hermann Goering, the flamboyant Commander of the German Air Force, who was known as *Der Dicke* – the Fat Man. Despite private reservations, he publicly professed himself as confident as his Führer. 'My *Luftwaffe* is invincible,' he declared. 'And now we turn to England. How long will this one last – two, three weeks?'

2
'A Large Party in Progress'
(10 July–16 August 1940)

Despite its losses in the Polish and French campaigns, the *Luftwaffe* was still superior to the RAF – indeed in the forthcoming battle the Germans outnumbered their opponents by about four and a half to one[11] – but its bombers, Stukas, and twin-engine fighters were vulnerable. The battle would turn on the conflict between the single-engine fighters – Willy Messerschmitt's quicksilver Me 109 against Sydney Camm's Hawker Hurricane and Reginald Mitchell's Supermarine Spitfire. The odds here were more even. Indeed, according to Richard Overy in his book *The Battle of Britain*, there were fewer German single-engine fighter pilots available than their Allied counterparts. The Me 109s would also be operating at the limit of their effective radius of action, their pilots having to keep a wary eye on their fuel gauges or risk ditching into the sea.

The sturdier Hurricane was the backbone of Fighter Command, far outnumbering the faster Spitfire, but it was the Spitfire that captured the popular imagination and, according to new research by Dilip Sarkar, destroyed an equal number of enemy machines. Everywhere it was seen, people simply stood and stared – bewitched – as they still do more than seventy years on. For the pilots who flew it, it was a case of love at first flight. Its Staffordshire-born designer had devoted the final years of his short life to its design, refusing all advice to rest while suffering from rectal cancer. When he died in 1937, aged only forty-two, it was just over twelve months after watching 'Mutt' Summers, Vickers' chief test pilot, fly prototype K5054 for the first time on 5 March 1936. He lived long enough, however, to learn that the Government had ordered 300 of the planes, and that at the insistence of Sir Robert McLean, Chairman of the company, it was to be called 'the Spitfire'. Mitchell thought it 'a bloody silly name'.[12] It was perhaps as well that he never knew that a child in Stoke-on-Trent was christened after the plane.

The first of 'the Few': R.J. Mitchell (2nd row, centre, in white shirt) at Queensbury Road Secondary School in Stoke-on-Trent, c.1903

Jeffrey Quill, Summer's assistant, was the second pilot to take her up on 26 March. The more he flew her, the more convinced he became of the aeroplane's 'immense importance'. Through hours of test-flying and – remarkably for a test pilot – several combat missions during the Battle of Britain with 65 Squadron – he and Mitchell's devoted team helped to ensure that the plane performed as Mitchell would have wanted. The fighter pilots who were to follow were awestruck by the 'clear-cut beauty, the wicked simplicity of its lines' and never forgot their maiden flight.

Richard Hillary, who was born in Australia but went to Shrewsbury School, recalled his own first flight after the outbreak of war: 'The machine was sweeter to handle than any other that I had flown. I put it through every manoeuvre that I knew of and it responded beautifully...I was filled with a sudden exhilarating confidence.'[13] For John Ashton too the Spitfire would remain by far his favourite aeroplane:

> It was the most delightful to handle of all the aircraft I have ever flown. The cockpit fitted like a glove and every control was easy of access. In a tight corner it behaved beautifully. At high speed it retained its manoeuvrability and it was just like a feather to handle. Even its shape was the most graceful of all fighter aircraft.[14]

'A Spitfire cockpit is small. It smells of metal and leather, of raw horsepower and excitement. Once in the sky a Spitfire pilot is alone, a hunter, an acrobat and a king.'
(William Ash, Under the Wire)

In the coming battle, the pilots of Fighter Command also had major advantages. In charge they had Air Chief Marshal Sir Hugh Dowding, lean as a whippet, to whom much of the strategic credit is due. They also had the benefit of a radar-based command and control system, a crucial factor in the outcome. (When Sir Robert Watson-Watt, who had developed the system of radar used in wartime Britain, gave the third Mitchell Memorial Lecture in Hanley, Stoke-on-Trent, in 1948 it was entitled 'Radar – the Complement of the Spitfire'.) Finally they were fighting over their own territory, which gave the battle a peculiarly intimate – even surreal – feel. WAAF plotters would sometimes find themselves monitoring an engagement in which brothers, boyfriends or fiancés were taking part. Harold Fenton, Commanding Officer of 238 Squadron, once found himself making a head-on attack on an Me 110 right on top of his own house at Hamble in Hampshire.

Dating the Battle is problematic as it had neither a definite beginning nor end, and both the French and Germans ascribe different dates from the ones now usually accepted by the British – the sixteen weeks from 10 July to 31 October 1940. Some fighter pilots believe that the battle over Dunkirk was the real beginning of the Battle of Britain; other pilots felt that the Battle never really came to an end. Rather unfairly, perhaps, the official dates exclude a number of pilots who distinguished themselves in the heavy fighting over France in May and June 1940 but were recovering from wounds or were otherwise engaged for most of the later period.

John Ashton was one; Gareth Nowell, who was born in Handforth, Cheshire, was another. He flew with 87 and 32 Squadrons until he was seriously wounded on 23 May. By then he was a notable ace and had received the DFM and bar. Newell Orton from Warwickshire was another of the most successful pilots in the Battle of France, whose fifteen victories with 73 Squadron brought him the DFC and bar. As he was instructing during the Battle of Britain, his name also does not appear in the official listing of Battle of Britain pilots nor on their monument. Orton did not live to see this – he was shot down and killed on 17 September 1941.

During the first phase of the battle, the *Luftwaffe* attacked Channel shipping and made massive fighter sweeps over south-eastern England, hoping to lure the whole of Fighter Command to its destruction. Warned of its intent by the Bletchley Park code-breakers, Dowding resisted the temptation and fought cautiously with very small units, but there were still too many casualties. Numerous pilots who successfully parachuted into the Channel drowned or died from hypothermia, for Britain had no proper air-sea rescue service until 1941. The Germans were better at rescuing their airmen; nevertheless, many of the latter carried pistols with them to ensure a swift end if they came down in the dreaded *Kanal*.

In spite of Dowding's reluctance to commit his forces to a war of attrition, the German plan was succeeding. By 19 July, his losses were rising at such a rate that Fighter Command seemed as if it would be wiped out within weeks. On that day alone he lost ten fighters, with five pilots killed and five wounded, against four *Luftwaffe* aircraft shot down. Hitler, more preoccupied with an invasion of the Soviet Union than Great Britain, now made his 'last appeal to reason'. Churchill ignored it. The German leader, who so far had apparently tried to bluff the British to the negotiating table, now authorised plans for an invasion to go ahead. The scheduled date for Operation *Seelöwe* – Sea Lion – was 15 August, later delayed to 15 September.[15]

In late July, No. 41 Squadron entered the fray. One of its most audacious and skilful pilots, George ('Ben') Bennions, was born in the Potteries and had attended the North Road Council School at Burslem (where his parents were caretakers) and then Longton High School. A passenger flight with Sir Alan Cobham in Stoke-on-Trent gave him an early taste for flying and, with his friend and school contemporary Ralph Carnall, he had enlisted in the RAF in 1929 as a 'Trenchard brat' (as the apprentices at the training school at Halton were known). But both yearned to fly and were eventually accepted on to a pilot's training course, qualifying as sergeant pilots in 1935. Carnall then became a member of 111 Squadron, the first unit to receive the Hawker Hurricane in 1937. He was in action over Dunkirk and was shot down for the first time on 10 July 1940, crash-landing at Hawkinge, but escaping unhurt. Bennions, after service in Aden before the war, was commissioned in April 1940 and made his first 'kill' by shooting down an Me 109 on 28 July.

Next day his squadron of eleven Spitfires again confronted more than 100 attacking aircraft over Dover, and while he was firing at one of the dive-bombers his own aircraft was hit. An Me 109 flashed past and Bennions followed. Although his port guns were all out of action, he fired three bursts from his remaining guns and saw the German fighter pull up into a vertical climb. Then his own machine was raked from behind and he had to break off and return to Manston. His flaps had been damaged and one tyre punctured so that when he landed his aircraft went spinning across the airfield. His Spitfire was a write-off.

George Bennions

August began quietly with bad weather hampering operations. This all changed on the 8th, when various squadrons were scrambled to intercept raiders attacking the convoy 'Peewit' as it neared the Isle of Wight. As they approached, they saw a large formation of Stuka dive-bombers with its fighter escort stepped above them. Although they were still three quarters of a mile away, a number of the more inexperienced pilots immediately opened fire, wasting some of their precious fifteen seconds' worth of ammunition. Within minutes a ferocious dogfight was taking place.

The battle was joined by 'Jas' Storrar flying with 145 Squadron. James Storrar's family had run a veterinary practice at Chester since the early 18th Century, and he was educated at Chester City and County School. In 1938, aged seventeen, he had joined the RAF by altering his birth certificate and was already a veteran in his teens, having been credited with eight 'kills'.

His most vivid memory was of the frantic day when he shot down a Stuka in the morning and an Me 109 in the afternoon. Turning for home, he saw another Stuka flying low for France. After firing one short burst he was out of ammunition but saw flames flicker from the other plane. They were now alongside and so close that he and the German pilot stared at each other. He recalled: 'I could see his face quite clearly. For the first time during the war I realised I was shooting down a man and not just an aeroplane. Suddenly the burning wing began to crumple and he turned over, dived into the sea and exploded.'[16] It was one of twenty-two planes lost by the Germans that day as against RAF losses of thirteen Hurricanes and Spitfires. Storrar's own squadron, however, had suffered particularly badly with five pilots killed in the one action. A few days later when his squadron was stood down, having lost ten pilots in five days, he was awarded his first DFC. Of the twenty-seven ships that made up 'Peewit' only four reached their destination; the remainder had been badly damaged or sunk.

Older than 'Jas' Storrar by several years but still a 'green young pilot' was 'Johnnie' Johnson, who admitted to pranging his first Spitfire four days after flying it for the first time. He was born in Leicestershire and studied at Loughborough College and Nottingham University. When he had tried to join the Auxiliary Air Force and the RAF Volunteer Reserve, he had been rejected, and it was only with the expansion of the Volunteer Reserve scheme prior to the outbreak of war that he was accepted and sent to Hawarden in Cheshire to train. That August he joined 616 Squadron, which had just been withdrawn from the battle.

What impressed him most, he told the author, was 'the astonishingly high morale of all concerned. There was never any suggestion that we might lose'.[17]

'Jas' Storrar (centre) with ground crew in front of a North American Mustang Mk 1V in 1945

However, a pre-war rugby injury, exacerbated by his recent accident, was causing him much anxiety while flying, and a few days later during an embarrassing meeting with his CO he was not only grounded but much to his chagrin suspected of a 'lack of moral fibre'. He jumped at the chance of an operation to solve the problem, but thereby missed most of the battle, particularly its second phase, which was about to begin.

The costly attacks that August were simply the prelude to *Adlerangriff* (Attack of the Eagles), the all-out air offensive designed to crush Fighter Command in a fortnight. It began on 12 August with a co-ordinated attack

24

on the British coastal radar chain. One WAAF who was tracking incoming aircraft suddenly realised what was happening. 'My God,' she cried, 'they're bombing us!' The station at Ventnor on the Isle of Wight was destroyed, but fortunately others were never out of action for more than a few hours.

That day too heralded the massive attacks on fighter airfields throughout southern England. Dennis Armitage, who worked as an engineer at Norton and Biddulph Collieries before the war, had also trained at Meir Aerodrome and had been commissioned when war was declared, joining 266 Squadron. Thereafter he had 'settled down to a long, lazy summer at Wittering, interrupted only by a rather abortive visit to Dunkirk'. But early in August the squadron flew their Spitfires south where they experienced an altogether different tempo of combat. With their orders changing by the hour, they ended up at Tangmere, en route to Eastchurch. Then, as he relates in a memoir, they were suddenly in action:

> We were told we might be called on to protect the aerodrome if necessary but under no circumstances were we to engage the enemy if we could possibly avoid it; it was important there would be a full squadron to go to Eastchurch…We went up to patrol base for the third time and after about ten minutes we were told over the RT [radio-telephone] 'There are enemy aircraft to the south but under no circumstances are you to engage them.' Then, after a brief pause, 'They are bombing Portsmouth – go to it.' So we went to it and had quite a field day, for the Germans had forgotten to send a fighter escort. One of the lads, however, did not come back.[18]

Armitage had accounted for one of the three bombers claimed by the squadron, but P/O Dennis Ashton had been shot down in flames. His body was found a month later by a naval minesweeper and buried at sea.

The squadron arrived at Eastchurch on 12 August. Next morning – 'Eagle Day' – it had a rude awakening. At 7.05 a.m. the German Commander Johannes Fink personally led his Dorniers on a low-level bombing attack on the coastal bases at Sheerness and Eastchurch, and Armitage woke to find his bed 'waltzing' about his room and the whole place shaking as if they were in the middle of an earthquake. Disentangling himself from a mass of bedclothes, plaster, window-frames and broken glass, he went to investigate and found six fellow pilots who had taken shelter in the enormous chimney in the Officers' Mess totally covered in soot – and the water supply had gone down in the raid! Fortunately the bogginess of the ground absorbed much of the explosions –'like letting off fireworks in an enormous jelly.' But the Operations Block had been put out of action and five Bristol Blenheim night fighters and a Spitfire had been destroyed. One of the ground crew's huts had also received a direct hit, killing a number of those sheltering inside.

Michael Crossley's 32 Squadron had seemed to be constantly in action that August, during which he claimed a dozen 'kills' with another shared and one damaged. He was also promoted to Acting Squadron Leader, awarded a Distinguished Service Order (DSO), and shot down twice, without injury. In his notes he gave a typically laconic account of the fighting of 12 August, during which he downed two more 109s:

Coo! What a blitz! Patrol base. All of a sudden we sight a cloud of Huns and move unwillingly towards them, but sight another cloud complete with mosquitoes a bit nearer; we move even more unwillingly towards them and attack. Everyone takes a swing at the 50 Dornier 215s and the Messerschmitt 109s. Hell of a lot of zigging. Very hectic. Day's bag nine 109s, three 215s.

The afternoon of 15 August was even more hectic, culminating in a raid on Croydon aerodrome by *Erprobungsgruppe* 210 led by *Hauptmann* Walter Rubensdörffer. Vectored to the scene, Crossley saw 'a large party in progress' and needed no second invitation to join in, charging at the masses of Me 110s which were so intent on dive-bombing that they did not see his squadron until too late. Croydon was put out of action for two days, but the Germans lost twelve planes with Rubensdörffer himself being one of those shot down. By the time the squadron was finally withdrawn from the battle later that month, Hitler had again postponed the date for the invasion to 17 September.

In *Luftwaffe* circles 15 August became known as Black Thursday. The Germans had flown nearly 2,000 sorties, Fighter Command 974. But the Germans lost 75 aircraft against 36 British. One of the casualties was the twenty-three-year-old Coventry man Sgt Frederick Bernard Hawley, whose Spitfire disappeared into the sea after combat with an He 115 off Dunkirk. Also in action that day was another pilot who was to have a long association with Stafford, Ernest 'Gil' Gilbert, a flight sergeant with 64 Squadron and a veteran of the French campaign. Mid-Channel his squadron tangled with 100 Me 109s and Gilbert promptly shot one down. Immediately he was fired on from behind. One bullet removed the coolant gauge from the dashboard, and alarmingly his cockpit began to fill with steam. Still under attack he broke for home, losing height rapidly towards Dover, whereupon his assailant fled. As he approached Hawkinge, Gilbert had the unnerving experience of having to land standing up in his cockpit with no air speed indicator.

Dennis Armitage's 266 Squadron had been re-posted to Hornchurch and was also heavily involved in the day's events. Armitage himself was fortunate to get back to base, his Spitfire severely damaged by cannon fire during an attack on a Ju 88 off Dover. In his memoir he vividly recalled the arena of the skies over the Home Counties with 'vapour trails of a scrap already in progress looking like a giant skein of white wool that a kitten has been playing with'. At first enemy formations appeared as 'just a long, thin, horizontal dark cloud on the horizon, and then as we approached it became a mass of little black dots'. Their attack brought chaos:

> For a minute or two there would be aeroplanes everywhere, Spitfires and Hurricanes and Me 109s above and below, to the right and left, all with throttles hard forward and sticks hard back, twisting and turning in a mad whirlpool. The carefully thought-out formation attacks which we had practised so long and assiduously were gone with the wind the moment the enemy fighters appeared. Soon you would find yourself going round and round in a tight circle with two or three Me 109s, and because the Spitfires had a slightly better turning circle you would gradually get the better of them, but just as you were getting your sights on they would flick onto their backs and dive away, and because they were quicker in the dive and there might be some more up in the sun waiting to dive on you, you did not follow. And then you would

look around for the rest of the party and for miles in every direction there would not be a single aircraft in sight.[19]

Dennis Armitage

The 'gentlemanly' attitude that had existed in the early part of the battle was changing as the fighting grew ever more savage. The 16 August proved traumatic for 266 Squadron, which lost four Spitfires with two pilots killed, including the CO, S/L Rodney Wilkinson. It was not so much his death as the manner of it that angered the surviving pilots, and Armitage recorded the change in attitude that this engendered:

> He was seen to bale out apparently unhurt but his body was found as full of holes as a sieve... Our 'Wilkie' was much loved and the thought that he was shot up while dangling helplessly from a parachute filled us with a vindictive hate which had not been there before.[20]

The machine-gunning of RAF pilots was apparently a reprisal for the British decision to fire on seaplanes carrying the Red Cross that the *Luftwaffe* was sending out to rescue their pilots downed in the Channel. Dowding himself felt that the Germans were justified in shooting at RAF pilots descending over England as they were still potential combatants, whereas Germans descending should be immune from being fired on as they were prospective prisoners of war. This cut no ice with some of the Poles, who gave no quarter to their opponents wherever they were. James Storrar recalled that when the recently captured *Oberleutnant* Runde was escorted into the squadron mess, a Polish officer took a shot at him there! There were also cases of German aircrew parachuting to safety only to be shot or beaten to death by the locals. Fortunate indeed therefore was David Blomeley, who also baled out that day. This time he was not fired on by friend or foe, though he did briefly end up in hospital before being posted as an instructor.

All across southern England the attacks continued, with Fighter Command facing almost suicidal odds. Residents of London and the Home Counties had a grandstand view and at times, unexpectedly, encountered the combatants. Some downed RAF pilots were seen returning to their stations by train or on the tube, sometimes carrying their packed parachutes. When Richard Hillary crash-landed in a cornfield near Lympne, he was immediately invited to join a cocktail party nearby.

Less welcoming, however, was the reception received by James Nicolson, who had trained at Ternhill. On 16 August, wounded in the foot and eye, and with his Hurricane ablaze, he was about to bale out when an Me 110 overshot him. He slid back into the blazing cockpit and continued to fire at it despite the searing heat. After he had finally baled out, severely burned, he was fired on by members of the Home Guard and further wounded by shotgun pellets. Whilst recuperating, he was awarded the Victoria Cross – the only such award made during the battle. Some pilots later felt that the award should have been given to Fighter Command itself in honour of all its pilots, just as the George Cross was awarded to the Island of Malta and its people in 1943.

Churchill, who had made a point of visiting front-line airfields, had met some of the pilots featured here. Now, watching the ebb and flow of the battle from the operations centre at Uxbridge, he was deeply moved. He may well have been reminded of Agincourt and the words spoken by Shakespeare's Henry V ('We few, we happy few, we band of brothers'). As they were leaving, he turned to his military liaison officer, Major General Ismay, and said, 'Never... has so much been owed by so many to so few'. The words, Ismay recorded, burned into his brain. A few days later when Churchill repeated them in the House of Commons, his words burned into the collective memory of the nation.

3
In the Balance
(18 August–7 September 1940)

The pilots themselves were sceptical of such myth-making and sometimes parodied Churchill's most famous line. One of them switched the two prepositions ('never... has so much been owed to so many by so few') and declared that it was a reference to their unpaid mess bills!

On Sunday, 18 August – known as 'The Hardest Day' – the Germans tried again to deliver a decisive blow with co-ordinated attacks against key airfields. Kenley and Biggin Hill were severely bombed. No sooner had Armitage's squadron followed orders to 'pancake Charlie 3' (to land at Manston) than a formation of Me 109s screamed past without warning, strafing the bomb-cratered airfield as they went. The last but one pilot to land made a dash for cover, tripped and fell, and then rolled along the ground with bullets kicking up the earth all around him. He took a single bullet in the arm. The last pilot down, the New Zealander Dick Trousdale, adopted a praying attitude – Mohammedan style – and was saved by his parachute, from which several bullets were later extracted. Around him two Spitfires were burning fiercely and another six were seriously damaged, leaving only three serviceable. The largely civilian staff had taken shelter in the labyrinth of caves under the aerodrome and simply refused to come out. At the end of the day Fighter Command had lost 68 fighters to the *Luftwaffe's* 69. One blow for the Germans was the forced removal of their former pre-eminent terror weapon, the Stuka, which the RAF was simply swatting out of the skies.

The numbers of Armitage's 266 Squadron kept on dwindling. The twenty-three pilots who went south had been reduced to nine so that everybody had to fly on every sortie without fail – and then they were under strength. After the Commanding Officer, they lost their senior Flight Commander – 'badly singed before he could get out of his blazing Spitfire' – and within a week Armitage had been promoted from Junior Flight Commander to Acting Commander. With it came 'the awful job of writing to parents or wives – not often wives – of the lads who had not come back. For several days there was at least one to do every night.'[21] He too did not escape unscathed, as he later recalled:

> Suddenly I heard a loud explosion, something hit me on my left leg, and there was a terrifying noise of rushing air. I whipped into a vertical turn, looking fearfully up towards the blazing sun and then, as confidence returned, I spotted what was probably the cause of the trouble diving away, already some 5,000 feet below. I realised the noise was simply due to the Perspex hood having been blown out by the explosion and, that apart, my machine seemed quite manageable. But my left leg was numb from the calf down. I put my hand down gingerly to feel if my foot was still there and, reassured on this point, I headed for home.[22]

Although hobbling about with a stick and having to be helped into his Spitfire, he continued to fly until the depleted squadron was ordered back to Wittering to reform. In less than a month after their baptism of fire began, they were down to five pilots.

Back in action with 501 Squadron, Ken Lee had made several claims that August but on the 18th, while returning to base, he was shot down over Canterbury by the German ace *Oberleutnant* Gerhard Schöpfel. Hit in the leg, and with his Hurricane on fire, he again had to bale out:

> I came wafting down in a cornfield. An old chap, with a military cap on, jumped up from the corn. He had a gun...I was just in shirtsleeves with no means of identifying myself. Consequently I was held at gunpoint until the London Irish arrived, who took me off to a local golf club for a refresher. My boot was soggy with the blood, like a Wellington you have got wet in a stream...We went in and I was given a brandy. There were all these people. 'You know old chap,' said one, 'I was on the fourth tee and this aircraft came so low it made me miss my stroke.'[23]

He did not fly again operationally until October, when he was also awarded the DFC. His citation read: 'This officer has led his section and flight with marked success. He has displayed great dash and determination and has destroyed at least six enemy aircraft.'

From 24 August to 6 September, the airfields of Fighter Command and the aircraft factories that supplied them suffered further devastation from the concentrated and sustained attacks of up to 1,000 enemy aircraft crossing the Channel daily. These included many more fighters, and losses on either side were about equal – 286 German planes to 275 British – which effectively meant that Fighter Command was losing. Even worse was the loss of experienced pilots, with another 103 killed and 128 wounded. During 1940 nearly 400 men of the RAF – mostly pilots of Fighter Command – were rendered incapable of active duty because of the burns they had suffered.[24] Richard Hillary was one – shot down in a mass of flames over the North Sea on 3 September and in the water for some time before being rescued by the Margate lifeboat. His face and hands had been terribly burned, and after initial hospitalisation in Margate he was transferred to the Royal Masonic Hospital in London. The first day there, when his dressings were being changed, an auxiliary nurse fainted.

Contrariwise, George Hassall Nelson-Edwards led something of a charmed life. He had been born at Stafford and, like Richard Hillary, attended Shrewsbury School and then Oxford University where he joined the Air Squadron. Consequently he was called up on the outbreak of war and eventually posted to 79 Squadron. He was committed to the battle that August and almost came to grief on one of his first sorties when his Hurricane was shot out of the sky and he crashed, though his injuries were minor. The following month he was again shot down, this time baling out into the Irish Sea. His luck still held and he was picked up by the SS *Dartford* to fight another day.

It was not only combat that was taking its toll. Accidents, engine failure and forced landings were commonplace, sometimes fatal. Numerous planes were last seen diving into the sea from 'unknown causes', the pilot probably unconscious from a defect in his oxygen supply. There were also cases of what is now euphemistically called 'friendly fire'. On 24 August, Hurricanes of No. 1 (RCAF) Squadron shot down a Blenheim by mistake. Its pilot was posted 'missing', its air-gunner – Daniel Wright of Lichfield – was killed. He was eighteen. Nowhere was safe. At Hawkinge aerodrome the funeral of a dead pilot was just ending when without warning a raid came in. The padre and mourners scattered instantly, with two of the deceased's fellow pilots jumping into the grave on top of his coffin as the bombs erupted around them.

The original Few were fewer. On duty from dawn till dusk, they were also haggard with exhaustion. Some fell asleep in their cockpits as soon as they landed; others slept through bombing raids on their airfields. Replacements were mostly untried and untested, their training cut to the bone. Many had never fired their guns or spent more than a few hours on operational aircraft. Nothing could have prepared them for the shock of their first combat – the panic, bewilderment and sheer terror, followed (if they were lucky) by jubilation as they came in to land, soaked in sweat, having survived for that sortie at least. Some cracked up; one was so traumatised by his initial combat experience that he couldn't remember his own name. Often they did not survive their first week – sometimes their first day. Sgt Oliver Houghton, of Foleshill, Coventry, joined 501 Squadron on 27 August and just over a week later was shot down and killed over Kent, his Hurricane plunging into Long Beech Wood. He was nineteen. Even years afterwards, Dowding could hardly bear to recall the intolerable stress and sorrow of those days and the 'pall of gloom' as each day's casualty figures came in.[25] Churchill later wrote that by the beginning of September the scales had tipped against Fighter Command.

Early that month Gerry Edge was given command of 253 squadron, which had lost three commanding officers and eleven pilots in three days. As he was enjoying a rare break, playing squash with his flight commander, an urgent recall went out. Still in their squash gear, they took off with seven other pilots to confront an approaching force of some thirty-six Ju 88s with an even more numerous fighter escort. What followed was, in the words of his number two,

John Greenwood, 'the most frightening attack he ever made', for they went in head on, line abreast, at a closing speed of 600 mph and he was unable to break right or left. At the last second he thrust the stick forward, and the enemy bomber went overhead by a few feet. Five German aircraft were lost, and the effect of such attacks on German morale can only be imagined. Some of their exhausted aircrew were baling out at the mere sight of a British fighter.

Others did anything to escape. Mike Cooper-Slipper's 605 Squadron had moved from Drew to Croydon, and over the next few days he shot down an Me 109, damaged two bombers, and shared in the destruction of a third. Another made a run for the Channel, jettisoning its bomb-load on the houses and fields below in a desperate attempt to increase its speed. A few days later Cooper-Slipper attended a social evening where he overheard an attractive young woman telling how she had nearly been killed by bombs from a plane being chased by a Hurricane. He introduced himself as the pilot and just over a year later they were married.

Also back in the fighting, 41 Squadron had left the relative calm of Catterick to relieve the over-stretched 54 Squadron at Hornchurch. The sight of the departing pilots, hollow-eyed, dishevelled and dog-tired, gave them an inkling of what lay in store. 'We really began to earn our pay then,' George Bennions later remarked (which for a young fighter pilot was 14s a day).[26] He and his fellow pilots were up at dawn, ready to make the four or five sorties of up to 90 minutes each before retiring, exhausted, and trying to sleep through the nightly barrage. Even when they were eating, transport was waiting outside the mess, ready to whisk them to their Spitfires at a moment's notice.

Another member of the squadron, Ronald 'Wally' Wallens, who had been born at Stourbridge in the West Midlands, recorded the events of one such day – 5 September – which 'started well for the squadron but was to end in a terrible shambles'.

By mid-morning the squadron was airborne at full strength, its twelve Spitfires intent on intercepting a large formation of Dorniers and Heinkels with an escort of about fifty fighters that was coming in over Gravesend:

> 'Robin' Hood, our CO, was leading and he detached 'A' Flight, under Norman Ryder, to give us cover against the 109s. I was petrified, but had to grin at the order – six Spitfires against so many 109s was a bloody tall order, but the imperturbable Norman calmly acknowledged it as he broke away. One would have thought he was being asked to take the bloody dog for a walk.
>
> In 'B' Flight I was as usual flying Number 2 back up to 'Robin'. I had been petrified earlier but now I was shitting blue lights at the sight of so many swastikas and black crosses. I was sticking like glue to 'Robin', waiting for his order to open fire, yet wishing like hell that he would call it off and come back tomorrow...I was flying almost level with 'Robin' on his right as he gave the order to fire. The concentrated fire of sixteen Brownings ripped into the bombers which emitted clouds of smoke and bits of metal and broke formation as 'Robin' and I broke rapidly to port, not waiting around to judge the results with 109s breathing down our necks.[27]

The bombers that had been attacked later crashed at Calais and St Omer and a number of the Me 109s had been shot down. The squadron had suffered only slight damage to one Spitfire.

The success of the morning was, however, eclipsed by a disastrous afternoon. Unable to gain height advantage and position in the time available, Wallens' Flight attacked a large force of bombers and fighters head on over the Thames estuary – 'a desperate manoeuvre that could age one prematurely'. Within seconds the six Spitfires were engulfed: two collided, and both pilots – one the Commanding Officer – were killed; a third pilot, whose machine was shot up, baled out.

Wallens had fired at the bombers and broken away violently. Below him he then saw two Me 109s and, with a long burst, destroyed one. As he lined up on the second, he was 'jumped' from above by a fighter that raked his Spitfire before he could react:

> The din was indescribable as the 109 cannon and machine gun fire tore great chunks out of my wings and blasted into the cockpit. My instrument panel disintegrated, my radio control disappeared, my armoured glass windscreen was scored on the inside but intact, and my leg went numb with a hammer blow that, strangely, did not seem to hurt at all as a cannon shell tore it apart.[28]

With his Spitfire now handling 'like a sack of coal', Wallens tried to bale out, only to find that his canopy had jammed. He had no option but to crash-land on Stifford Clays Farm in Essex, rocketing across one field, smashing through a fence, hurdling a ditch 'like a Grand National winner' into another field and coming to rest in a great cloud of dust in the shelter of a large tree. Gerald Winch, a local farmer, watched from his tractor as he worked in a nearby field, meaning to go and investigate when he had finished. But then he saw a motor cycle going towards the crash and decided not to bother. After all it was nothing out of the ordinary for the time. Wallens, despite his serious leg wound ('a ghastly mess of blood and mush'), had been fortunate indeed: one bullet had removed his helmet's right radio ear-phone, another the face from his wrist watch. But for the rest of the Battle he would be merely a spectator. It was to be many weeks before he was allowed out of bed to go solo in a wheel-chair.

Ronald 'Wally' Wallens

*

The third phase of the conflict began with the *Luftwaffe* extending its bombing of urban targets, especially London. This change in strategy had perhaps been provoked by retaliatory raids by Bomber Command on Berlin, which started on the night of 25/26 August. Goering, who had promised the German people that such raids would never happen, was ridiculed; Hitler was incensed. In a ranting speech on 4 September, he threatened to raze British cities to the ground. He also openly renewed his threat of invasion: 'In England they're filled with curiosity and keep asking "Why doesn't he come?" Be patient. Be patient. He's coming! He's coming!' In a later broadcast, Churchill retorted: 'We are waiting for the long-promised invasion. So are the fishes.'

On the afternoon of 7 September, Goering, described by one of his own pilots as 'looking like a great dumpling',[29] watched at the Pas de Calais as a huge armada of 350 bombers escorted by 617 fighters thundered overhead on their way to the East London Dock area. It was to date the largest raid in the history of aerial warfare. Twenty-one British squadrons were scrambled or at readiness, but for once the switch in targets caught the controllers by surprise and many *Luftwaffe* pilots flew to London relatively unopposed. At Duxford the controversial idea of a 'Big Wing' under Douglas Bader was tried out for the first time, but it was slow in forming up and made a fairly inconclusive debut, apart from filling the sky with planes. Dennis Armitage, who later flew with the wing, considered it 'not a great success'. Ken Wilkinson, from Cheltenham, who had spent his career so far as 'tail-end Charlie', watching the backs of the men in front who were 'doing the heroic things', also flew with the wing but found that by the time it arrived on the scene the Germans were usually well on their way home.

That day the German pilots were jubilant, describing the East End as 'an ocean of flames'. The dead numbered 448 with a further 1,337 seriously injured – and that was only the first day. The ruthless bombing went on throughout the night from 8 p.m. to 4.30 a.m. – as it would for many weeks to come. The Blitz had begun.

Tommy Hicks, then a four-year-old boy who lived near the docks in Bermondsey, witnessed the terror bombing. He recently recalled how one evening when shopping with his mother and baby sister in the Old Kent Road the sirens suddenly started their shrill demented wailing and sent everyone scampering to the nearest shelter. As they were crossing the road, a truck careered at them out of nowhere, just missing Tommy but hurling his mother and the pram into the air. The youngster stood transfixed, hearing only his mother's screams as the searchlights sliced through the dark and the guns opened fire, the first bombs already whistling down to light up and devastate adjoining streets. In the lottery of survival his mother lived, his sister died.

4
Achtung, Spitfire!
(15 September–31 October 1940)

Donal Rock West had been born in Staffordshire in 1921
and seemed destined to follow his father into the world of
banking, but the tedium of office work was too much for
his adventurous spirit. After only a few weeks, he walked
out of the bank and into the nearest RAF recruitment office.
After training as a pilot and still in his teens, he was posted
to No.141, a night fighter squadron flying Defiants. In 1940
he joined 256 Squadron and his first combat missions were
in the night skies over the capital and then Liverpool,
during which he destroyed a Ju 88 and an He 111. Even the
enemy seemed appreciative of his skill. After downing one
aircraft, he went to visit the luckless pilot in hospital. The
German gave him a thumbs up and said 'Good shot.'[30]

Hitler's decision to bomb London and other cities was a
godsend that allowed the squadrons of Fighter Command a
precious breathing space in which to repair their airfields
and regroup. More fighter squadrons were also made
operational. At the beginning of September, two Polish
squadrons and a second Czech squadron were combat-
ready. They were to fight with such ferocity that the Polish
303 Squadron would become the most successful unit of
Fighter Command, destroying 126 enemy planes for the
loss of nine of its own pilots. Dowding later paid tribute to
the 'unsurpassed gallantry' of the Poles which he felt had
had a direct bearing on the outcome of the battle.

As usual, Bennions with 41 Squadron was in the thick
of the action and did not escape unscathed. On 6 September
he belly-landed at Rochford. On the 11th, another day of
frantic activity, he was wounded in his left heel by a shell

splinter from one of the escorting fighters whilst attacking a Dornier 17. It was so painful that he couldn't move his foot, and when he looked down he saw that his shoe was full of blood. He force-landed at Hornchurch where a doctor extracted the splinter and stitched him up. Within days he was back in action and living up to his reputation of being an outstanding pilot and a crack shot, as a typical combat report demonstrates:

> After the commencement of the engagement, I found myself about 2,000 feet below a section of 5 Me 109s. Two of the Me 109s dived down onto me and I evaded by turning sharply right; then one dived away and as I turned to follow three more came down on me. After turning and twisting violently, I spun out and, on pulling out, I found that one only had followed me down. I turned to engage and he disappeared into the clouds. I climbed back to 15,000 feet and sighted a loose formation of four Me 109s circling. I attacked the rear one from the inside of a left hand turn and, after a short burst, I saw pieces fly off the aircraft, which then rolled over and spun inverted for about 8,000 feet and then dived straight into the ground midway between Canterbury and Herne Bay, near a very large wood.

His score continued to rise with seven confirmed 'kills' – all fighters with the exception of one bomber – and numerous probables. His achievements were recognised on the 19th by the award of the DFC, his citation reading: 'Pilot Officer Bennions has led his section with great distinction. He has destroyed seven enemy aircraft and possibly several others. His determination and coolness have had a splendid influence on his squadron as a whole.' Among the letters of congratulation he received was one from Mr M.V. Gregory, headmaster of his old school, Longton High.

Even this impressive record was about to be overshadowed by that of a fellow officer, the redoubtable Eric Lock. 'Lockie' (or 'Sawn-Off' as he was known because of his short stature) had been born in 1920 at Bayston Hill, near Shrewsbury, and joined the RAFVR at the Potteries' Aerodrome at Meir in February 1939. With war imminent, he was commissioned as a Pilot Officer and posted to 41 Squadron at Catterick, North Yorkshire, where he did nothing in particular for the early part of the battle. It was not until 15 August that he made his first 'kill', when the Germans launched an attack from Norway with sixty-three He 111s, escorted by twenty-one Me 110s. They were savaged and repulsed by various squadrons over north-east England, and Lock opened his score by despatching one of the Me 110s.

However, he truly came into his own when the squadron was posted to Hornchurch, the forefront of the battle in the south. On 5 September alone he shot down four German planes in the action described above by 'Wally' Wallens. His combat report details the encounter:

> I was flying in formation with the rest of the squadron when we intercepted a formation of enemy aircraft. We attacked the bombers first…It then developed into a dogfight.
>
> I then engaged an enemy He 111 which I followed down until it crashed into the river. I climbed back to 8,000 feet and saw an enemy He 111 which had left the main formation. I engaged same and set his starboard engine on fire. I closed in to about 75 yards and fired two long bursts and smoke came from the fuselage. The enemy aircraft then put his wheels down and started to glide. I stopped firing and followed him down. I was then attacked by an Me 109 who fired at me from below and wounded me in the leg. As he banked away he

stall turned. I fired at him and he exploded in mid-air. I then followed the bomber down until it ditched on the sea about 10 miles from the first one in the mouth of the river.

On only his second engagement Lock had become an official ace. Within the week he had destroyed eight enemy planes – a feat that resulted in the award of his first DFC on 1 October. His second came only three weeks later after he had downed fifteen aircraft in nineteen days, during which he had been wounded and had had to bale out three times. Six more 'kills' were to follow, making him the highest scoring RAF pilot of the Battle of Britain.[31]

Eric Lock

*

Derbyshire-born Henry 'Butch' Baker, also with 41 Squadron, had arranged his marriage for 15 September but had to postpone it as Hitler had other plans. That Sunday – now celebrated as Battle of Britain Day – two major attacks were launched that were intended to finish off Fighter

Command and break the morale of Londoners once and for all. The invasion (if it were still deemed necessary) had been rescheduled for 21 September. Forewarned by the code breakers, Dowding and Air Vice-Marshal Keith Park (the only two RAF commanders who received Ultra intelligence) were aware of the German strategy and made their preparations accordingly. By chance Churchill was again visiting the operations room of No. 11 Group at Uxbridge where Park, the tall, spare New Zealander who was so brilliantly orchestrating the defence of London and the South-East, had just remembered that it was his wife's birthday and that he had forgotten to buy her a present. The Prime Minister watched from above as the busy plotters pushed their discs to and fro, and more and more red bulbs went on to show various squadrons engaging. Soon they were all fighting. Churchill turned to Park. 'What other reserves have we?' he asked. 'There are none, sir,' came the reply.

In the mêlée of twisting and turning planes, the pilots of 41 Squadron came well up to the mark. Henry Baker shared in the destruction of an He 111, while George Bennions shot down an Me 109 and damaged a Do 17. 'Lockie' meanwhile was even more successful, as his combat report narrates:

> I saw a Hurricane attack Me 109s, so I joined him. He shot one down in flames as I was attacking. I attacked from behind and underneath, firing a rather long burst. He went into a vertical dive on fire. The Hurricane pilot then beckoned me to attack the three Dornier 17s, so we selected one each. We both delivered an astern attack, to stop the rear machine gunner; this seemed rather effective...When I delivered my second attack, the starboard engine burst into flames and the aircraft

dived into the sea. By now the two other Dornier
17s had dived to sea level. We carried out a quarter
beam attack on the remainder. After a while, the
starboard engine caught fire and he also landed in
the sea by a convoy. But this was shot down by the
Hurricane…I left the other Dornier being chased by
the Hurricane as I had no ammunition.

Also out of ammunition was Mike Cooper-Slipper with
605 Squadron. With his Hurricane critically damaged by a
Dornier's return fire in a running dogfight over Surrey and
Kent, he finally rammed the bomber and sent it crashing
into a field near Maidstone. Three Germans parachuted to
safety, but Cooper-Slipper struggled to escape as his
canopy refused to open. Finally, with his plane spinning
down out of control, he managed to slide it back and bale
out, tearing off several fingernails in the process. Then he
lost consciousness. When he came to, he found his
parachute had somehow opened and he floated down to
land at Church Farm, Marden. He returned to his Croydon
base in an army vehicle via a children's party and several
pubs.

One of the most celebrated episodes of that day was
when Buckingham Palace came under attack. The
Canadian Keith Ogilvie of 609 Squadron, one of a number
of Commonwealth pilots who had been stationed at RAF
Meir in early 1940, shot up one of the attacking bombers,
as he recorded in his combat report:

We were ordered to attack a large formation of
Dornier 17s, with a heavy Me 109 escort. In getting
in position I saw a lone Dornier separated from his
formation. I went for it and gave it several bursts
from the beam. The fire was returned. Two other
Spitfires attacked, and on my next attack I could see

fire in the Dornier's cockpit. As I went beneath it I saw two men jump and their parachutes open. The whole disintegration [was] a most amazing and terrifying sight. The enemy aircraft spun and broke in half and dropped somewhere around Battersea.

Keith Ogilvie (3rd from right) with fellow pilots of 609 Squadron at Middle Wallop after their 100th kill.

The main part of the aircraft crashed in the forecourt of Victoria Station and the tail unit landed outside a Pimlico pub to the great joy of its patrons. Meanwhile the two German aviators had landed on the Oval. One of the other attackers was Cheshire-born Ray Holmes of 504 Squadron, who had finished off the plane by ramming it. His Hurricane came down in Buckingham Palace Road, Holmes having baled out. (He landed in a dustbin.) Each of the fighter pilots was credited with a third of a 'kill'.

The crews of the 200 German bombers, told that the RAF was down to its last fifty fighters, had found themselves without their escort as they reached the outskirts of the capital, so fierce had been the opposition. One crew member described the bombers as 'hanging over

London like ripe plums'. There, waiting for them, was the awesome sight of Douglas Bader's 'Big Wing' of sixty fighters from Duxford. Although militarily less effective than Keith Park's preferred strategy of sending fewer squadrons into action over a longer period, psychologically the effect on the Germans was devastating. The planes of the 'almost extinct RAF' were everywhere. Badly rattled, the German force was soon streaming in disarray back to France with British fighters having to queue up to shoot at them.

That afternoon the second attack was launched with similar results. Goering's wish to draw Fighter Command into a great air battle had at last been fulfilled – though the outcome was different from what he had expected and from what was claimed. As usual in such engagements, pilots of both sides greatly overestimated their success. *The Times* reported that the RAF had shot down 175 planes for the loss of 30 British fighters; the *Völkisher Beobachter* announced that the *Luftwaffe* had shot down 79 British aircraft for the loss of 43 of their own planes.[32] In fact the Germans had lost 56 planes with 20 more damaged; British losses totalled 28. Nevertheless, over just one week the German Air Force had lost 298 aircraft and many of its most experienced airmen. The scales had tipped once again – this time decisively in Fighter Command's favour. As he left the operations room, Churchill personally thanked the WAAFs who had been on duty. 'Well done, young ladies,' he said. 'This has been a most memorable day. You will tell your grandchildren about it one day.'

Bomber Command continued its relentless attacks on the invasion fleet being assembled in harbours all over occupied Europe. Guy Gibson, later to achieve fame and a

Victoria Cross for the Dam Busters' Raid, described 'the Battle of the Barges':

> On that night [15 September 1940] we made our biggest raid on Antwerp... Many barges were sunk, many blew up, destroying others around them. They were full of stuff and we could see, there and then, there was no doubt about it, the Germans were ready.
>
> Flying low around those docks that night we could easily see the tanks on board, the guns on mountings at the stern of each invasion craft, the tarpaulins over sinister objects on the docks. '*Der Tag*' was drawing near for the Hun, and September 15th was, perhaps, the day when they realised that it would be no use.[33]

Two days later, on 17 September, Hitler postponed his invasion plans indefinitely.

*

The Blitz on London continued, however, and there were still days of intense fighting. On 26 September, Gerry Edge was shot down over the Channel when his Hurricane was hit from behind and burst into flames. Although suffering from burns, he managed to bale out and was picked up by a motor-boat nine miles off Dungeness. Thereafter the battle entered its final phase when the mass daylight raids that were proving so costly virtually ceased and were largely replaced by high-level sweeps by fighters and fighter-bombers. Realistically, the Spitfire was the only plane with the speed to catch them. On 1 October, having been at the forefront of the Battle of London for a month, George Bennions was about to go on leave. Then a scramble was ordered to intercept a force of Me 109s north of Brighton. His Spitfire was armed and ready and so he joined in, hoping to add to his personal count of eleven enemy aircraft confirmed.

After a skirmish with a number of fighters, the squadron was returning to base when Bennions saw a group of Hurricanes being bounced by about forty Me 109s. In an act of selfless gallantry, he swooped to help, riddling the rearmost plane which burst into flames. Immediately his own Spitfire was hit and a cannon shell exploded in the cockpit, taking out his left eye and knocking him unconscious. When he came to, he found the aircraft in a screaming dive and decided to bale out even though he could not see the altimeter. Unable to move his right arm, he pulled the stick with his left hand, rolled the aircraft over, released his Sutton harness and fell out, somehow managing to pull his ripcord. Then he passed out again. Miraculously he survived. He came to in a field at Dunstalls Farm, told the farmer who he was and lapsed into a coma.

His left eye had gone and there was a hole through which his brain was exposed. After emergency treatment, he was transferred to the Queen Victoria Hospital, East Grinstead, where he was treated by Archibald McIndoe, the New Zealand-born pioneer in burn management, who in 1939 had been a consulting plastic surgeon to the North Stafford Royal Infirmary in Stoke-on-Trent, Bennions' native city. Simultaneously, Bennions had become a member of the Caterpillar Club, for people whose lives have been saved by parachute, and a member of the Guinea Pig Club, as the patients of McIndoe were known. But he was, as he later admitted, at a very low ebb, so low that for a time he felt that the future could hold nothing for him.

Then a friend in another ward asked him to go along. Bennions later recalled what followed:

> I was on crutches at the time but I managed to get over there with a hell of a lot of struggle and self-pity. As I opened the door in Ward 3 I saw what I can only describe now as the most horrifying thing I had ever seen in my life. That was this chap who had been badly burnt, really badly burnt. His hair was burnt off, his eyebrows were burnt off, his eyelids were burnt off, you could just see his staring eyes. His nose was burnt, there were just two holes in his face. His lips were badly burnt. I looked down at his feet also. His feet were burnt.
>
> I got through the door on crutches with a bit of a struggle. This chap started propelling a wheelchair down the ward. Halfway down he picked up a chair with his teeth. That's when I noticed how badly his lips were burnt. Then he brought this chair down the ward, threw it alongside me and said, 'Have a seat, old boy.' And I cried. I thought, 'What have I to complain about?' From then on everything fell into place.[34]

The 'chap' was his school friend Ralph Carnall, who had been shot down in flames on 16 August over Kent. Carnall was to remain a patient at the hospital for over a year and eventually returned to flying. For the five weeks that he was there, Bennions was treated so skilfully by McIndoe that few people would ever notice any disfigurement. But he never flew in combat again.

Sgt Pilot Cyril Babbage on the other hand was one of those pilots who seemed to have nine lives. He had been born in Ludlow, Shropshire, in 1917, and flew with 602 Squadron during the Battle. In the shooting gallery of August he had made four 'kills' but had been forced to bale

53

out into the sea on the 26th and was fortunate to be picked up by the Bognor lifeboat. In September he claimed three more 'kills' at the cost of serious damage to the Spitfires he was flying, but always managed to fly them back for repair. His final engagement in the Battle was on 12 October when he attacked a Ju 88. So badly shot up was his own aircraft by return fire that he had to attempt a forced landing near Lewes, during which the plane overturned. He walked away unharmed.

Night attacks against London and other cities were still intense, but daylight activity during the latter half of October gradually petered out. Although it was not known at the time, and although the air battles continued, the Battle of Britain had been won – or at least it had reached stalemate, with the Germans losing 1,887 aircraft to the RAF's 1,023 (excluding the losses of Bomber and Coastal Commands). Many of the *Luftwaffe's* most experienced aircrew were now in prisoner-of-war camps or their graves. The German military cemetery on Cannock Chase in Staffordshire was to be the only part of the United Kingdom that they would ever occupy.

Britain had survived by virtue of the heroism and sacrifice of 'the Few' or 'Dowding's Chicks', as Churchill called them, teenagers and young men from every social class. But they had been sustained by the Many, who also played their part in the battle: by Bomber and Coastal Commands which attacked the invasion ports night after night; by the workers who, under the dynamic management of Lord Beaverbrook, turned out twice as many fighters as their German counterparts; by the ground-crews, the plotters, the radar operators, the observer corps, the repair teams, the Post Office engineers and NAAFI girls, many of whom were in the front line. Indeed, a number of the

WAAFs were awarded the Military Medal for their exceptional bravery under fire. As the fighter pilot William Ash put it: 'People can soar as well as any Spitfire'.[35]

The Battle of Britain was the first time that Nazi power in Europe had been checked, and Fighter Command was victorious simply by surviving and denying the air superiority to the Germans that they needed for an invasion or for a decisive bombing campaign. Churchill ranked it alongside the most critical victories in British history, such as the Armada and Trafalgar. Its significance cannot be overstated, for it was also the Battle of Europe. In 1960, when the official Russian history of the war described the Battle of Britain as no more than a 'smoke-screen', Sir Keith Park commented: 'Russia was literally saved by the Battle of Britain. If we had not disposed of the trained formation leaders of the *Luftwaffe*, Russia would have been steam-rolled in 1941 as Poland was in 1939.'[36] Without Britain, America may also have stayed out of the war and there would have been no base from which to launch Operation Overlord – the D-Day liberation of Europe – in 1944.

After the defeat of Germany, Field Marshal von Rundstedt, the German Commander in the West, was asked to name the crucial battle of the Second World War. His captors expected him to say 'Stalingrad' or 'Normandy', but he replied: 'The Battle of Britain.'[37]

5
So Much Owed

Of the nearly 3,000 Allied pilots who were awarded the Battle of Britain clasp after having flown at least one authorised sortie, 544 were killed and many others severely wounded. Another 795 were subsequently killed, among them Hugh Sharpley, Geoffrey Roscoe, Thomas Wood Savage, Kenneth Gray and Allan Sydney Dredge.

Hugh Sharpley, of Hanchurch, was the younger son of the Town Clerk of Stoke-on-Trent and worked as an engineering assistant for the Staffordshire Potteries Water Board. He was the complete all-rounder: an excellent marksman, a spirited horseman who had won several steeplechases, a prominent member of the North Staffordshire Polo Club and vice-captain of the Swynnerton Cricket Club. He had taken up flying in 1935 when he joined the aero club at Meir and was soon one of its star performers. As a member of its General Committee and Flying Committee he helped with the formation of the Civil Air Guard at the aerodrome and later joined the RAFVR there.

After war was declared, he was made operational as a Sergeant Pilot with 234 Squadron. He survived the Battle of Britain but on 16 November 1940 he failed to return from a sortie. A fellow pilot, the notable ace Bob Doe, remembered what happened in a letter to the author: 'I can recall Sgt Sharpley as a quiet pleasant person, but as he was in the other flight I did not know him well. I believe that he crashed into the sea off Newquay.'[38] Sharpley was thirty and his body was never recovered. In February 1944, his brother, Major Roger Sharpley, was lost at sea whilst serving with the East Africa Force. Both men are remembered on the war memorial that stands in Trentham cemetery.

Geoffrey Roscoe (known generally as 'Pete') was the son of Colonel and Mrs H. Roscoe of Primrose Hill, Hanford, and was an old boy of Newcastle High School. He was well known in the area as a member of the Stoke-on-Trent Rugby Club and Swynnerton Cricket Club (where he would have met Hugh Sharpley). Before the war he had been a mining student and was commissioned in the Royal Engineers (Territorial Army) before transferring to the RAF in February 1940. After completing his training as a fighter pilot, he served briefly with 79 Squadron in September 1940 and then with 87 Squadron from 8 October onwards, taking part in the latter stages of the Battle of Britain.

Geoffrey Roscoe

He was subsequently promoted to Flight Lieutenant and, in January 1942, he married Miss Anne Brock, daughter of Air-Commodore H. M. Le Marchant Brock of Bushy Heath. Only weeks later, on 24 February, he was killed in a flying accident. He was twenty-five. At his funeral at Carmountside Crematorium, the many mourners included a guard of honour of fellow pilots and Battle of Britain veterans. One of the chief mourners was his younger brother, Second Lieutenant Alan Roscoe. Described as 'a lad of most charming personality [who] was universally popular', he too had been a pupil at Newcastle High School before going up to St John's College, Oxford, where he obtained a BA degree. At first he was in the Oxford and Buckinghamshire Regiment but then transferred to the Army Air Corps in which he obtained his wings and served as a glider pilot. He was killed a few months later in June 1942, aged twenty-one.

Their eldest brother, Lieutenant Ken Roscoe, had been with the BEF in France and was taken prisoner in 1940 at Boulogne (where he won the Military Cross). He spent most of the war in German prison camps until he managed to escape in April 1945. On his return to Hanford a fortnight later the streets were decorated with bunting to welcome him home. He went on to have a distinguished academic career and in 1968 was appointed to the first Chair in Soil Mechanics at Cambridge University. He was killed in a car accident two years later. In February 2007, the 65th anniversary of Geoffrey's death, a plaque was unveiled in his honour at St Mathias church, Hanford, in the presence of his eighty-one-year-old sister, Mrs Mary Fielding, his sole surviving sibling.

Thomas Wood Savage had been born at Burslem, Stoke-on-Trent, in 1920. After being educated at Wrekin College, he returned to his home town to join the printing firm of Messrs Warwick and Savage, in which his father and uncle were partners. Before the war he was an active member of the Civil Air Guard and qualified as a pilot (probably at Meir Aerodrome). In April 1939, he also joined the RAFVR and was called up on 1 September. After more training he was posted to 64 Squadron in time to take part in the final phase of the Battle of Britain. He was then posted to the Middle East where he served as a Flight Lieutenant with 92 Squadron, taking part in the successful operations from El Alamein to Tunis. He was killed in action over Sicily on 10 July 1943 during the invasion of that island, probably by 'friendly fire'. He was twenty-three and is remembered on the Malta Memorial. A year later he was awarded a posthumous Mention in Dispatches for his distinguished service, during which he was credited with four enemy aircraft destroyed and several damaged.

Kenneth William Gray, of Basford, Newcastle-under-Lyme, joined 85 Squadron at RAF Castle Camps in Cambridgeshire on 16 September 1940 and took part in the final weeks of the Battle of Britain. Commissioned in June 1942, he was killed on 9 June 1944 as a Flying Officer with 25 Squadron. He was twenty-three and he is remembered on the Runnymede Memorial for those with no known graves.

Unluckiest of all, perhaps, was Allan Sydney Dredge, another volunteer from Foleshill, Coventry. In the Battle of Britain he flew with 253 Squadron and was credited with four victories. More operational sorties followed in 1941 when he served with 261 Squadron on Malta. There, outnumbered by enemy fighters, he was shot down and badly burnt, returning home for treatment as another of McIndoe's 'guinea-pigs'. In 1943 he was awarded the DFC and promoted commander of 3 Squadron, leading which he destroyed six V1 flying bombs and struck at a wide range of enemy targets, as the citation for his DSO (awarded in December 1944) relates:

> Shipping, airfields, locomotives and various other targets have been most effectively attacked. Throughout these operations, S/L Dredge has displayed inspiring leadership, great courage, and determination, qualities which have contributed materially to the successes obtained.

On 18 May 1945, the then Wing Commander Dredge was engaged in plane trials at Farnborough, Hampshire, when he was killed in a flying accident in a Mosquito. The European war had ended just over a week before.

*

Despite its savage losses, the RAF ended the Battle of Britain with more pilots available than it had at the start. So much so that some of them were not made operational until after the battle was over. One such pilot was Roylance Mills Chatfield, whose father was formerly the licensee of the Jolly Potters Inn at Hartshill in Stoke-on-Trent. Educated at Newcastle High School, he was later on the staff of Lloyds Bank at Uttoxeter before he enlisted in the RAFVR in May 1939. On the outbreak of war he qualified as a pilot and was commissioned in October 1940. Rapid promotion followed. Before he was twenty-two he was promoted to Flying Officer and a year later to Flight Lieutenant. Having just missed the Battle of Britain, he was posted overseas in 1941 and saw service in the Middle East and Mediterranean war zone with 73 Squadron.

On 14 June, while strafing Gazala airfield, his Hurricane was shot down by intense flak and he was captured. Managing to escape, he then trekked 25 miles to safety, a journey that took him ten hours. He thus became a member of the exclusive Late Arrivals' Club, whose badge, a blue and white enamel winged flying boot, signified that most of its holders had walked back from behind enemy lines. In 1944 he was awarded the DFC, his citation reading:

> This officer was engaged on fighter operations in the Western Desert for a period of 18 months and remained in Tobruk during the early siege. On his second operational tour, he took part in many day and night fighter attacks during which he destroyed two enemy aircraft, bringing his total victories to at least three hostile aircraft destroyed. F/Lt Chatfield is now serving as a transport captain [with 267 Squadron]. He took an active part in the recent operations at Salerno and Cos. At all times he has completed his allotted tasks with keenness and skill, displaying great courage and devotion to duty.

After the war he was involved in the Berlin Airlift and then commanded 234 fighter squadron in Germany. He retired from the service in 1959.

*

Of the few of 'the Few' featured in this account, none was killed during the Battle of Britain though two – Richard Hillary and Eric Lock – were lost later in the conflict.

After months of painful reconstructive surgery on his face and hands, Hillary persuaded a Medical Board to pass him fit and he was posted to train as a night-fighter pilot at RAF Charterhall in the Scottish Borders. Whilst on a training exercise in the early hours of 8 January 1943, his Blenheim spiralled out of control and exploded on impact. What was left of him was cremated and the ashes scattered from a Spitfire over the Thames estuary and the Strait of Dover.[39] His account of the Battle *The Last Enemy,* published in 1942, became a best seller.

Eric Lock crash-landed, badly wounded, on 17 November 1940 and ended up in a hospital ward opposite Richard Hillary. In addition to the two DFCs he had already won, he was awarded a DSO on 17 December 1940. After a lengthy stay in hospital, during which he underwent fifteen operations, he was promoted to Flight Lieutenant and returned to operational duties with 611 Squadron. He was posted 'missing' on 3 August 1941 when he failed to return from a fighter sweep over France. A fellow pilot, W. G. G. Duncan-Smith, believed that he was shot down into the harbour at Boulogne by intense anti-aircraft fire. Consequently he has no known grave, but his name lives on in 'Eric Lock Road' in his birthplace near Shrewsbury and in the 'Eric Lock Bar' at the Shropshire Aero Club. His final tally of twenty-six confirmed enemy aircraft destroyed (and a further eight probables) makes him one of the top-scoring pilots of the war.

John Ashton was awarded the DFC in March 1941, his citation crediting him with at least five victories. He later served in Egypt and Malta and in 1944, as commander of 73 Squadron, he led sorties over Italy, Yugoslavia and Austria. At the end of the war he had flown over 500 operational sorties and had more than 3,600 flying hours to his credit. After leaving the RAF he became Chairman and Managing Director of the electro-plating company Beck and Moss in Hanley, Stoke-on-Trent. He continued to fly as an instructor, helping to train young Air Force cadets at

RAF Shawbury, and he was an active member of the Wolverhampton Aero Club, twice competing in the King's Cup Air Race. He was also a member of the Bugatti Owners' Club, in which he was involved both as an official and competitor in rally and hill-climbing events. In 1969, as Chairman of the Appeal Fund, he was instrumental in securing a Spitfire for permanent display in Hanley. He died in 1988 and is buried in Whitmore cemetery.

The Stafford men all survived the war. After his period as an instructor, David Blomeley retrained as a night fighter-pilot and was posted to 605 Squadron in 1943 when he flew the Mosquito VI, destroying several more enemy aircraft in the latter part of that year and being awarded the DFC. He remained in the service until he retired in 1958 as a Squadron Leader. He died in 1991.

Gerry Edge recovered from his injuries and returned to operational service in November 1940 as Commanding Officer of 605 Squadron before being posted overseas. He ended the war as a Group Captain credited with twenty 'kills' – although his true score was probably higher. He was awarded the DFC in 1940 and an OBE in 1945. After the war he farmed in Kenya but returned to live in Worcestershire in 1963. He died in 2000.

Mike Cooper-Slipper, still aged only nineteen, was awarded the DFC in November 1940 'for displaying great skill and daring in air combat'. He joined 135 Squadron and was posted to the Far East where he shot down five Mitsubishi G3M bombers in the desperate defence of Singapore. Later he was taken prisoner by Japanese paratroopers but escaped on foot, travelling miles through the jungle and eventually reaching Java. After a period of convalescence in India and South Africa, he commanded an experimental high altitude fighter unit in North Africa and took part in several high altitude combats with German reconnaissance aircraft until his health began to break down again and in 1944 he returned to England. He ended the war as a test pilot at RAF Lichfield with up to ten 'kills' to his credit. When he left the RAF in 1946, he emigrated to Canada where he became chief test pilot for Orenda Engines Ltd. He died in 2004, aged eighty-three, the lady whom he had met during the Battle of Britain, his wife of sixty-three years, by his bedside.

After surviving the Battles of France and Britain, 'Gil' Gilbert was promoted to Pilot Officer and spent most of the war as an instructor, based for some time with 21(P) Advanced Flying Unit at Wheaton Aston, near Stafford. George Hassall Nelson-Edwards took command of 93 Squadron in 1942 and saw further action in North Africa, during which he claimed a string of enemy aircraft destroyed or damaged. At the end of his tour in 1943, he too was awarded the DFC. He retired from the service in 1960 with the rank of Wing Commander.

In 1942 Michael Crossley was posted to act as a test pilot in America and promoted Wing Commander later that year. Upon his return to the UK in 1943, he contracted tuberculosis, which ended his operational career. After the war he was awarded an OBE and left the RAF to become a tobacco farmer in South Africa. He died there in 1987, aged seventy-five. In the months in which he was fighting, he claimed twenty victories, making him one of the outstanding aces of the conflict.

Byron Duckenfield returned from Japanese captivity at the end of the war and remained in the RAF until 1969, retiring after thirty-three years' service as a Group Captain.

A fluent Japanese speaker, he then worked in marketing for Rolls-Royce in Japan before finally retiring to Bretby Park, Burton-on-Trent, where he lived for three decades before his death in 2010, aged ninety-three. At his funeral his coffin was met by an RAF guard of honour and entered Bretby crematorium to the sound of Glenn Miller's *Moonlight Serenade*.

Ken Lee was posted to the Middle East in December 1941 and with 260 Squadron took part in the Battle of El Alamein the following year, claiming his 7th and last victory on 10 November 1942. He was then given command of 123 Squadron in Iran and brought it back to the Western Desert in May 1943. On 3 July of that year, he was shot down for his third and final time during a raid on Crete and became a POW at Stalag Luft 111 where he helped with preparations for the Great Escape. He survived the appalling forced march from the camp and was liberated in May 1945, leaving the RAF in the same year as a Squadron Leader. He then worked for many years in Africa and Dublin before retiring to Spain. He finally returned to the UK to live in Sheffield and died in his nineties in 2008.

George Bennions eventually recovered from his serious wounds and was then given a limited non-operational flying category. Despite having only one eye, he eventually flew Spitfires again on limited flights and was mentioned in despatches in 1943 for his distinguished service. He was later posted to North Africa and Sicily to command the Ground Controlled Interception Unit which was to operate on Corsica after it had been invaded. However, in October 1943, while his landing craft was approaching Ajaccio, it was bombed and he was again wounded, necessitating a return to the Queen Victoria Hospital for further treatment.

He left the RAF in 1946 and became a teacher of technical drawing, metalwork and woodwork at Risedale School in Catterick, where a street in the village was named in his honour. He died in 2004, aged ninety.

The medals of George Bennions. His DFC is on the left and next to it the 1939-45 Star with Battle of Britain Clasp. The box contains his Caterpillar Club badge.

His school friend Ralph Carnall was commissioned in 1942 and in 1944 was posted to Calcutta with 684 Squadron. He remained in the RAF after the war at Fighter Control Branch until his retirement in 1963 as a Squadron Leader. He died in 1984, aged seventy-one. A plaque commemorating the two pilots was unveiled at Longton High School in Meir in April 2007.

Cyril Babbage was awarded the DFM in October 1940 and commissioned the following month. In 1941 he joined 41 Squadron and claimed his final 'kill' on 18 September of that year when he shot down one of the first FW 190s, flown by the German ace *Hauptmann* Walter Adolf, who was killed. Babbage remained in the RAF after the war and retired in 1964 as a Wing Commander. He died in 1977.

In June 1941, Dennis Armitage was given his own squadron – No. 129 – and received the DFC from the King 'for gallantry, leadership and flying against overwhelming enemy aircraft during the Battle of Britain'. On 21 September 1941, during a fighter sweep over France, he was forced to bale out and was taken prisoner. After numerous escape attempts, he was sent to Colditz where he wrote a play with Douglas Bader based on their POW experiences which was staged at the 'Q' Theatre in London for a two-week run in 1945 and later broadcast by the BBC. After the war he returned to Macclesfield and his former career as an electrical engineer in the Staffordshire coal mines. He also became Chairman of the Lancashire Aero Club until 1953 when he gave up flying. He subsequently moved to Petersfield in Hampshire where he died in 2004.

Ken Wilkinson led a charmed life and survived the Battle of Britain without a scratch. He saw further action during the war and also spent several spells in instructing. He left the RAF in November 1945 as a Flying Officer and then became a quantity surveyor. He now lives in Solihull.

Tony Pickering, the raw replacement pilot, joined 501 Squadron in August 1940 and was shot down shortly afterwards though he baled out unhurt. He rejoined the battle and then, after a period as an instructor, he served in the Middle East. He was released from the RAF in December 1945 as a Squadron Leader and now lives in Rugby.

'Johnnie' Johnson, the young pilot twice rejected by the RAF who was also suspected of a lack of moral fibre, later flew as Number 2 to Douglas Bader in 616 Squadron and became the highest scoring RAF fighter pilot to survive the war with thirty-eight 'kills' – almost all of them against the formidable Me 109 and FW 190. He flew over 1,000 combat missions, yet only once was his Spitfire hit by enemy fire. He ended the war with many decorations, including three DSOs and two DFCs, and retired after further service with the rank of Air Vice-Marshal. In 1969 he founded and ran the 'Johnnie' Johnson Housing Trust, a charitable association providing housing and care for the elderly, the disabled and vulnerable young people. He lived in Buxton, Derbyshire, until his death in 2001.

In 1943, after a prolonged convalescence at the RAF Rehabilitation Unit in Torquay, 'Wally' Wallens was given an upgraded category that allowed operational flying – but only in the UK – and he was posted to No. 277 Air-Sea Rescue Squadron at Hawkinge, which he eventually commanded. Here he flew Spitfire and Walrus search aircraft and was instrumental in rescuing a number of Allied airmen, once landing in the middle of a minefield to snatch a downed pilot from the sea. In 1944 he was awarded the DFC for his service both as a fighter and rescue pilot. After the war he worked in the motor trade and also ran several pubs and hotels, including the Seven Stars (now the Lamplighter) in Stratford-on-Avon. When he died in 1995 aged seventy-nine, RAF Brize Norton provided a bearer party in his honour.

After protecting London during the Blitz, Donal West served as an instructor before re-joining 256 Squadron in 1943 when he was posted to Malta to guard the Mediterranean shipping convoys. In 1944 he claimed another Ju 88, though his own Mosquito was shot up during the action. He rose to the rank of Squadron Leader and in September 1944 was awarded the DFC for his valour and devotion to duty. While overseas he met his future wife who was working for ENSA (Entertainments National

Services Association) and to whom he was married for 63 years. After the war he remained in the RAF and took part in the Berlin Airlift of 1948 before becoming a commercial pilot and setting up homes in the Bahamas and on Majorca. After the death of his wife in 2004, he returned to North Staffordshire to live at Penkhull, Stoke-on-Trent. He died in December 2012, aged 91.

Donal West and his wife Jo on their wedding day

Keith Ogilvie, who defended Buckingham Palace, was awarded the DFC in 1941, a few days after being shot down over France. He had been hit twice in the arm, once in the shoulder, and had lost a considerable amount of blood. He was in hospital for nine months and then sent to Stalag Luft III at Sagan. In 1944 he took part in the Great Escape and was one of the fortunate few not to be murdered by the Gestapo on his recapture. After the war he served with the

Royal Canadian Air Force until his retirement in 1962. He died in Ottawa in 1998, aged eighty-three.

Ray Holmes, who also defended the Palace, resumed his career as a journalist after the war. In 2004 he watched as parts of his Hurricane were excavated for the Channel 5 documentary *Fighter Plane Dig – Live!* and was happy to handle the joystick he had last held 64 years before. Its gun button was still set to 'Fire'. When he died a year later, flags flew at half-mast in his honour in the Wirral and his widow received a message of condolence from the Queen.

'Jas' Storrar went on to serve in various theatres of war, including the Western Desert. In 1944, at the age of twenty-three, he became Wing Commander of three squadrons of Mustang fighters charged with long-range escort duties. In this role they took part in the celebrated Mosquito attack on the Gestapo Headquarters in Copenhagen on 1 March 1945 and the attack on Hitler's Berghof at Berchtesgaden a few weeks later. At the end of the war he had twelve confirmed 'kills' to his name, a Bar to his DFC, and the Air Force Cross. He continued flying and was the last commanding officer of 610 (the County of Chester Auxiliary Squadron) before it was disbanded. His younger brother recalls how he used 'to frighten Chester to death – he flew under the Grosvenor Bridge in a Hurricane and said himself that he had never seen the flag pole of Chester Cathedral so close.'[40] He retired from the RAF in 1957 to become a veterinary surgeon and joined the family practice in Chester. He died in 1995, aged seventy-four.

James Nicolson, VC, was killed on 2 May 1945 when the plane in which he was travelling crashed into the Bay of Bengal. His body was never recovered.

Archie McIndoe was knighted in 1947 for his services to plastic surgery. Exhausted by his work, he died in his sleep in 1960, aged only fifty-nine, and his ashes were buried in St Clement Danes, the only civilian to be interred in the 'RAF church'. A year later a new burns research unit was established at the Queen Victoria Hospital and named the Blond-McIndoe Unit in his honour. The Guinea Pig Club of his former patients continues to meet annually.

Archie McIndoe with members of the Guinea Pig Club

The youngster Tommy Hicks survived the Blitz to become Britain's first rock-and-roll star under the name of Tommy Steele. He progressed to a career in films and stage musicals and, now in his seventies, he is still performing.

Lord Dowding, the overall commander of the battle, was retired in November 1940 after much intriguing against him by some of his fellow air marshals. The official history of the Battle of Britain made no mention of him. However, he lived long enough to see himself portrayed by Laurence Olivier in the 1969 film *The Battle of Britain,* and on his death a year later his ashes were placed in Westminster Abbey. In 1988, a statue of him was placed in front of St Clement Danes with the inscription: 'To him the people of

Britain and of the free world owe largely the way of life and the liberties they enjoy today.'

The other unsung hero of the battle – Air Vice-Marshal Sir Keith Park – was also treated shabbily in the aftermath of the Battle, although he was eventually reinstated and suitably honoured. When he was awarded a KCB (his second knighthood as he was already a Knight Bachelor), one of his colleagues sent him the message: 'Admiring congratulations. Twice a Knight at your age.'[41] In 2010, the 70th anniversary of the Battle of Britain, when a statue of him was unveiled in central London, Air Chief Marshal Sir Stephen Dalton, Chief of the Air Staff, said that he was 'a man without whom the history of the Battle of Britain could have been disastrously different'.

As a result of his premature death, Reginald Mitchell – the 'first of the Few' – was never fittingly honoured by his country. However, the debt owed to him was recognised by ordinary people in a 2003 poll conducted by BBC TV's *Midlands Today*, when an overwhelming majority voted him 'The Greatest Midlander of All Time'. Shakespeare came second.

NOTES

[1] *Evening Sentinel* Battle of Britain Supplement, 15 September 1990.

[2] *Ibid.*

[3] *Evening Sentinel,* 5 June 1940.

[4] Steve Darlow, *Five of the Few* (2006), p.15.

[5] *Ibid.*

[6] Len Deighton, *Battle of Britain* (1980), p.71.

[7] *Daily Telegraph* obituary of S/L 'Dimsie' Stones, 25 October 2002.

[8] Reported in Alan Brown, *Airmen in Exile* (2000), p.18.

[9] *Hansard,* 18 June 1940.

[10] Quoted in Martin W. Bowman, *Scramble* (2006), p.18.

[11] Stephen Bungay, *The Most Dangerous Enemy* (2001 ed), p.107.

[12] Gordon Mitchell, *R.J. Mitchell* (1986), p.130.

[13] Richard Hillary, *The Last Enemy* (1956 ed), p.64.

[14] *Evening Sentinel* Supplement, 28 October 1957, p. IV.

[15] David Irving describes Hitler's 'gigantic bluff' in *Göring* (1989). Churchill was not deceived and, according to Tim Clayton and Phil Craig in *Finest Hour* (2001 ed), felt that there was no significant invasion threat at that time whatever he said in public.

[16] From a telephone interview with the author.

[17] From a telephone interview with the author.

[18] *Squadron Leader Dennis L. Armitage, DFC* (1989), p.4.

[19] *Ibid.* pp.13-14.

[20] *Ibid.*

[21] *Ibid.* p.12.

[22] *Ibid.* pp.19-20.

[23] Darlow, *op.cit.* p.43.

24 E.R. Mayhew, *The Reconstruction of Warriors* (2004), p.45.
25 Dowding's Foreword to Alan Deere's *Nine Lives* (1991 ed).
26 Geoffrey Wellum, *First Light* (2003), p.194.
27 R.W. Wallens, *Flying made my Arms ache* (1990), pp.131-2.
28 *Ibid.*
29 'Blitz – Bombing and Total War', Channel 4, 15 January 2005.
30 *Sentinel*, 9 January 2013.
31 RAF Battle of Britain Memorial Flight Official Yearbook (2012), p.21.
32 Bungay, *op. cit.*, p.332.
33 Guy Gibson, *Enemy Coast Ahead* (1998 ed), p.97.
34 From a transcription of a sound recording of an interview with Bennions held by the Imperial War Museum.
35 William Ash, *Under the Wire* (2005), p.281.
36 Quoted in the *Evening Sentinel*, 1 August 1960.
37 Quoted in Martin Davidson & James Taylor, *Spitfire Ace* (2004), p.219.
38 Letter to the author, 31 March 2007.
39 Sebastian Faulks in *The Fatal Englishman* (1997) reports that at Charterhall the story went round that they had to fill his coffin with sand.
40 *Chester Chronicle*, 3 September 2004.
41 Recorded in H.A. Fenton, *Aquarius: A Flying Memoir 1928-1945*, p.103.

PART TWO

SERGEANT ERIC BANN
AND 238 SQUADRON

1
'Our Local Cobber Kain'

Samuel Eric Bann was born in Macclesfield in June 1914, the son of Samuel and Credence (née Wood) who had married in 1912. Maurice, their second son, followed in 1919, on whom Eric would keep a brotherly eye for the rest of his short life.

He was educated at Athey Street School and was also connected with St Andrew's church[1] and other organisations in the town, including the 20th Macclesfield Scout Group. He then progressed to Manchester College of Technology where he studied aeronautical engineering and, after passing his exams with honours, took a course of lectures at Sheffield Training College. He returned to Macclesfield and was associated with his father's sheet-metal business before going to work at the Fairey Aviation Company. He became a prominent member of the Macclesfield Aeronautical Society and resumed his attendance at St Andrew's. He was a popular and well respected figure in the community, never more so than after the outbreak of war when, according to the *Macclesfield Courier*, he was 'the hero of all the air-minded boys in the town' and 'our local Cobber Kain'.[2]

In May 1938, he had enlisted in the RAF Volunteer Reserve and completed his initial training as a 'weekend' pilot at No. 28 Elementary and Reserve Flying Training School at Meir Aerodrome in Stoke-on-Trent. With the German invasion of Poland on 1 September 1939, he was immediately mobilised there and the following month sent for more advanced instruction to No. 6 Flying Training School (FTS) at Little Rissington, near Oxford. At Christmas he received a welcome gift from the Lord

Mayor's Comforts Fund, which he acknowledged early in the New Year:

> Apart from the acceptability of the contents, the receipt of the parcel was a renewal of the links with my native place and it is very gratifying to know that, whilst the exigencies of service in the RAF keep me a considerable distance from Macclesfield, the borough at this season of the year has demonstrated its interest in all normally resident in the town who are now serving in the Forces.[3]

At the end of January, he received another gift and expressed his appreciation of 'the grand way' in which the people of Macclesfield had supported the Fund. 'The cigarettes,' he wrote, 'will help me pass away many weary hours of patrol duty.'[4]

Eric Bann and his wife May on their wedding day

During this period he met a Birmingham girl, Agnes May Butler (known as May), whom he married on a special 48 hours' leave in March 1940, with Maurice acting as best man. He may also have met Gordon Batt at this time, for both attended the same flying school. Batt had been born in Wolverhampton in 1916 but grew up in Coventry when his father started work at the Daimler factory. Despite being educated at Bablake School and the Coventry Technical College, Batt's academic achievements were by his own admission 'virtually nil'. He had taken up an engineering apprenticeship with Daimler and didn't think he stood much of a chance when he applied to join the RAFVR in 1938. After an initial problem with his medical (he was one tooth short for a fit person!), he was accepted and received his initial training on Avro Cadets at Ansty, a grass airfield to the east of Coventry. Like most of the Volunteer Reserve, he flew at weekends and during the evenings (weather permitting), except for two nights a week when he had to attend lectures on the Theory of Flight, Navigation, Meteorology, Armaments, Signalling and King's Regulations. After the outbreak of war, he was posted to Little Rissington and practised firing his guns for the first time over Portland Bill. Some months later it was there that he fired his guns in earnest when he first encountered the enemy at exactly the same spot.

*

At this stage many pilots were sent straight from training school to squadron and thus it was that in mid-May 1940 Bann and Batt were attached to 253 Squadron at Kenley at the height of the Battle of France. It was one of the most torrid periods in the history of the squadron; indeed, the French Air Force always maintains that the Battle of Britain really began at this time, with all fighter squadrons fully stretched from dawn to sunset. No. 253 had been split into two flights, with 'A' Flight (led by Guy Harris) flying to France on a daily basis from 17 to 23 May, while 'B' Flight (commanded by Harry Anderson) was stationed at Lille.

Gordon Batt

In a letter to the author, Guy Harris gave this account of the events of 18 May 1940, the day that Bann arrived at the squadron:

> The short history of 'A' Flight commenced in accordance with Dowding's ruling that no more complete squadrons were to be sent to France but composite squadrons were to be made up and go over for the day. Thus on 18 May, six aircraft from 253 at Kenley joined with six from 111 at Northolt

led by S/L Thompson and left very early for Vitry to operate from there for the day. After a pretty hectic day, nine of our Hurricanes were lined up ready to return when we were attacked by low-flying Ju 88s and six of our aircraft were destroyed. S/L Thompson decided that he, I and a sergeant pilot should fly the remaining three home, leaving the remaining six pilots to find their own way back. Which they did.

The following day a similar procedure was followed, only the twelve of us took off from Hawkinge after lunch for an offensive patrol over France/Belgium. I have little idea where as we had no maps, but we ran into a large force of He 111s escorted by Me 109s. In the ensuing mêlée I received a bullet in the back but managed to fly back to the coast and land at an aerodrome which turned out to be Dieppe. From here I was eventually carried on to a hospital ship at St Nazaire two weeks later – thanks to the Army.[5]

In a second letter he added that he did not return to the squadron and so had 'no knowledge of what took place after that date. We had a lot of casualties so there would have been a number of replacement pilots.'[6] Bann and Batt were two of them, but as Batt had injured his hand playing rugger he did not participate in the action. He did, however, carry out some 'local flying' in a Hurricane on 19 May, and Bann may have been doing the same before being called upon to help out. According to the Air Historical Branch (RAF), he took part in some of the daily flights: 'It appears that he was not actually stationed in France but was attached to 253 Squadron for flying duties to and from France for a few days in May 1940.'[7] The wording suggests that this was always meant to be a temporary arrangement.

Batt, reduced to a spectator, witnessed the return of what was left of the squadron after only a few days' fighting: '[It] arrived back in dribs and drabs, very bedraggled, extremely tired and a little demoralised.'[8] Each flight had lost half its pilots, including both Flight Commanders and the Commanding Officer, and, faced with the seemingly unstoppable German onslaught, what was left of the squadron was hurriedly withdrawn to England. Planes that were not airworthy were broken up with axes, and the leftover aircrew had to make their own way back through Boulogne. It was impossible for the squadron to continue and it was sent to Kirton-in-Lindsey in Lincolnshire to rest and reform. Meanwhile Bann and Batt were posted to RAF Tangmere, near Chichester, to join 238 Squadron that was being hastily reformed there.

Throughout this fraught period in our history, Bann wrote to tell his parents of his experiences. His letters, sometimes dashed off in odd moments between flights, provide a compelling insight into what it was like to be in the thick of the action, for events are described soon after they happened and not 'recollected in tranquillity' many years later. He adopted a jaunty tone whenever possible (to allay parental fears), although there was little hope of disguising some of the events that were unfolding, especially the squadron's ever-increasing number of casualties. He knew that his own chances of survival were slim and told Maurice as much, asking him to take care of May if the worst happened.

The letters originally appeared in 1988 as a duplicated booklet produced by the Macclesfield Historical Aviation Society. Some of them have since been reproduced in studies of the Battle of Britain, but they are now once more given in their entirety to make them more readily available.

Together, they provide a brief, poignant account of 238 Squadron's role in our 'finest hour'.

Bann obviously wrote many more letters than the twelve reproduced here – an article entitled 'Here is a Macclesfield RAF Hero' that was published in the *Macclesfield Times* in August 1940 mentioned 'dozens' of them and quoted from several, including brief snippets from two that do not appear in the booklet but which are included here. None of the letters to May, his young wife, was ever published. She eventually remarried, with the blessing of Maurice and his family, and died in the 1980s. Whether any of his letters still exist is unknown, for Maurice feared that they were 'lost or destroyed'. Even those on which the booklet was based are untraceable, for Maurice could not find them and had no recollection of their ever having been returned.

The twelve letters have been lightly amended where necessary, annotated, reordered and placed in context. Dates have been standardised, with some dates suggested for letters where they are missing. Other dates have been changed, for inaccurate dates have occasionally been added by an unknown hand before or during transcription. Other relevant documents have been added at appropriate points.

*

The first letter was probably written at Kenley as Bann was about to depart for Tangmere to join 238 Squadron (which he did on the same day). It summarises his experiences with 253 Squadron from 18 to 21 May. When the author sent a copy to Guy Harris, he wrote back: 'His letter is the only one I have seen describing the hectic events of those few days.'

[Letter 1]

Tuesday 1.15 p.m.
21 May 1940

Dear Mother and Father,

At last we are able to get time off for a letter or two.

How are all of you at home? I trust very well. Have been moving from place to place, so have never heard from anyone at home or Birmingham.

Have been having a real rough time, lost nearly all my clothes and been sleeping in any old place, plus getting into some real hot places.

Have been posted down to Tangmere to help form a new squadron. My old squadron pulled in every pilot in the last raid, even including the CO[9], and we came back almost halved in number. So we just can't carry on the squadron.

We have bagged about 40 German planes in the last four days, but their numbers are terrific – have been going in for about six of us to 40 and 50 of theirs. The air was thick.

I think we lost the flight commander yesterday. What a nice chap. They said he was engaged by about 10 fighters and went down fighting madly.[10]

Our squadron have been flying every day and we are very tired, plus on top of that, we have had orders to stop the advance at all costs. Believe me, to see the German dive bombers in their hundreds cutting at our poor troops makes you only glad to help. It's terrible.

Please do not send parcels or letters because of my constant change of address.

Been flying Hurricanes and Spitfires. What about that Father?

Cheerio for now,

With God's good grace I might be seeing you all one of these days.

Your Son
Eric

2
Green as Grass
(12 May–20 June 1940)

Tangmere, part of No. 11 Fighter Group, had been thoroughly modernised at the start of the war. From 12 May onwards, pilots and other personnel for the new squadron began arriving there.[11] Some were young and, by their own admission, 'green as grass'. The Welshman Charles Davis had had his course at Cranwell cut short in order to hasten his arrival. He was nineteen but he was not the youngest officer, for Brian Firminger was still eighteen. One of those with previous squadron experience was Sgt Henry Marsh (known as 'Tony') who had joined the RAF as an Aircraft Apprentice at the age of eighteen in 1928. He passed out of RAF Halton as a Fitter in 1931, later becoming a Sergeant Observer. Afterwards he had volunteered to train as a pilot and had received his initial instruction at RAF Perth and then at No.2 Flying Training School at RAF Brize Norton from January to October 1939. Subsequently he was posted to 253 Squadron where, according to an occasional diary he kept, it seems he was at his happiest.

He became best friends with his fellow sergeants John Anderson ('Andy') and Gilbert Mackenzie ('Mac') and in their free time 'the trio' enjoyed some 'very jolly' outings, not to mention some heroic pub crawls. 'Lord knows how we got back to camp,' Marsh (the driver) recorded after one such excursion. 'I've nasty memories of mounting the curbs on alternate sides of the road.'[12] Life lost some of its zest, however, when Andy was put out of action in April 1940. His Hurricane seized up and he had to bail out. 'Andy came down a bloody mess,' wrote Marsh. 'His R/T [radio telephone] cord stayed in the cockpit and the resultant jerk caused it to lacerate his face badly.'[13] He was hospitalised and the trio temporarily became a duo.

Mac had his own aerial adventure in early May when he sensed that something was wrong with his aircraft – a Fairey Battle – as soon as he had taken off. He then saw an airman who had missed the signal to 'let go' sitting on the tail plane. He immediately returned to the aerodrome where the 'tail squatter' was removed, shaken but unharmed.

On 9 May, the squadron moved from Northolt to Kenley and the following day the phoney war suddenly became very real, as Marsh noted: 'Germany invaded Holland and Belgium and we considered our long-awaited war had begun. Our co-squadron left for France, leaving us to defend the sector. At least we felt "in it".'[14] Long hours became the order of the day and there were 'no more nights out'. Everyone was thinking of France and how they would shape up there. Then out of the blue Marsh was posted.

On the eve of his departure, a reunion of the trio was arranged which almost never took place. Their Flight Commander appeared and told them that three pilots were urgently needed for France. In the event, however, with Andy still officially on sick leave and Marsh about to be transferred, it was decided that three others should go and the trio swiftly left for a few beers before going to the show *Shepherd's Pie*. Afterwards Andy left for home. It was the last time that the three of them would meet.

The next day, 14 May, Marsh had a final cigarette with Mac, who was 'a bit cut up'. Marsh himself was 'damned near to tears, and before going out of sight that last wave made my eyes wet'. He drove off in 'Frances' (his car) together with P/O John Urwin-Mann who had also been posted to the new squadron.

Urwin-Mann had been born in British Columbia in 1920, though his family returned to England two years later. They had set up home in Hove in East Sussex and John was educated at the Xaverian College at Brighton before joining the RAF in 1939. After training, he too had joined 253 Squadron. John Greenwood, the sole surviving member of the squadron from that time, recalled him for the author: 'I remember my friend 'Urinal' Mann (that was his nickname), a Canadian, full of fun. He joined 253 at Manston at the same time as we received Hurricane Is; he moved to Northolt and then Kenley where he left us just before our flight left for France on 15 May. (He never got to France.) We had many a beer together.'[15] So too did Marsh and Urwin-Mann, for en route to their new posting they stopped at Reigate where Urwin-Mann looked up some friends who owned a pub. Five hours later they continued to make unsteady progress, and after calling at several more hostelries Marsh finally arrived at Tangmere. 'That's the end of 253 Squadron for me!' he wrote. 'I'm down here with a new bunch, 238, as an 'old hand' to form the nucleus. It means a cushy job, no France for a while, decent bed, bath, food and accommodation – but no trio!'[16]

More 'old hands' followed the day after with the arrival of Stuart Walch and John Kennedy. F/Lt Walch had been born in Hobart, Tasmania, in 1917 and educated at the prestigious Hutchins School from 1927–34 where he proved to be an all-round sportsman. After leaving school he joined the family business, J. Walch & Sons, which sold books, stationery, musical instruments and sporting goods. In 1935 he joined the 40th Battalion (Militia) in which he served until he enlisted in the Royal Australian Air Force in 1936. He trained at the Flying School at Point Cook before transferring to the RAF in 1937 when he was granted a short service commission as a Pilot Officer for five years on the active list. In January 1938, he joined 151 Squadron at North Weald in Essex and became well known for taking less experienced pilots under his wing. Then, in May 1940, he was appointed Flight Commander (B Flight) of 238 Squadron.

Stuart Walch

F/Lt 'Jack' Kennedy was born in Sydney, Australia, and educated at St Charles' School and then Waverley College. At first he studied accountancy, but knew that a desk job was not for him and enlisted in the air force in 1936. From then on his career ran parallel to that of Stuart Walch, for he too graduated from Point Cook (where the two men may have met) and transferred to the RAF in the same year. In the *London Gazette* of 20 September 1937, their names appear in the same list announcing short service commissions. In December 1937, he joined 65 Squadron at Hornchurch and remained with it until his posting to 238. Both were twenty-three years of age.

So new was the squadron (it was considered to have come into being only on 16 May) that when some of those arriving asked where it was, they received the reply 'Never heard of it'. By 18 May it at least had a Commanding Officer when 30-year-old Cyril Baines appeared. A graduate of the RAF College at Cranwell in 1930, he had first been posted to 32 Squadron at Kenley and then joined 209, a Flying Boat Squadron, before returning to Cranwell as an instructor in 1935. He would help knock the embryonic squadron into shape during the first two months of its existence before he was posted to the Middle East in July 1940.

Marsh was still feeling the wrench of leaving his former squadron. 'I'm with a bunch of old and new pilots to form a squadron as we formed 253 last October,' he wrote. 'All that over again – but alone. I haven't been out yet. Don't want to, without Mac and Andy. Everyone else seems so damned foolish and unintelligent. Maybe we will be together again. God I hope so.'[17] He knew that 253 was 'fighting like hell' in France, evidence of which appeared in the form of one of their Hurricanes. It had been found abandoned at Dieppe and patched up by a desperate pilot who then flew it to Tangmere. The bullet-holed and splintered plane must have been a sobering sight for the pilots assembling there, even more so for Marsh.

On 21 May, he heard of 'two young pilots who were with 253 for a day or so before coming to us' and sought them out, eager for news. The two – Bann and Batt – told him that Mac was 'missing in action'. Marsh was surprised by his reaction:

> I didn't feel so cut up as I'd have expected. In fact I accepted it quite casually and resignedly. I'd rather hoped that Mac had meant more to me but then I suppose I'm the only thing that matters to me at all.[18]

Though he continued to hope that Mac would turn up, he eventually learned that he had been killed on 19 May and buried in France.

The squadron was in the process of being equipped with Spitfires and Marsh had been one of four pilots who had been collecting them during the previous week. 'As yet I'm not prone to do anything daring with them,' he wrote. 'I'm not the type anyway.'[19] According to 238's Operations Record Book (ORB), only one pilot of the first intake had flown Spitfires, and accidents were therefore not uncommon. Ironically, considering his caution, Marsh had 'the doubtful honour' of damaging their first plane by tipping it up and bending its propeller. The CO was not best pleased and Marsh found himself rested, with 'reams of reports to make out'.

Then he was suddenly summoned to the CO's office. Expecting another dressing-down, he was surprised to discover that two Hurricane pilots were urgently required and he and Urwin-Mann were the most eligible. 'At first I felt quite jittery,' he noted, ' – France and Mac's footsteps, but I became easier later on and was soon unconcerned again except for how I was to dispose of my kit.'[20] However, the weather subsided to the 'in abeyance' state and no more was heard of the affair. It was Marsh's third reprieve from the debacle taking place in France.

In the meantime there were many niggling problems to be dealt with that were no doubt typical for a squadron in its early stages of formation. At the end of May, the ORB recorded:

> Establishment 16 +5 A/C [aircraft]. Strength fully equipped – Nil. Personnel – 11 officers arrived, 17 allowed. Airmen – 157 arrived against 137 allowed. Strength for Flying Practice, 16 A/C which have been fitted with guns, rear armour and reflector sights. 4 A/C have R/T but batteries and accumulators are insufficient for the remaining A/C. 140 guns received, but the fire and safe mechanisms are deficient. No Cine Guns have been received. Only 8 out of 16 starter trolleys have been received.

Pilots continued to be accident-prone as they strove to achieve operational readiness. On 31 May, F/O MacCaw crashed his Spitfire, while on 2 June Hurricane 6600 was damaged and sent by road to Air Services at Hamble. On 5 June, Sgt Alsop landed a Spitfire without having the undercarriage accurately locked. The following day Sgt Gardiner crashed while manoeuvring into position for a take-off in formation when his Spitfire passed into the slipstream of another and tipped its nose, causing the airscrew to hit the ground.[21] On the 9th, F/O MacCaw came to grief again, colliding with a harrow that was being dragged by a tractor working on the airfield. Next day F/Lt Kennedy's Spitfire was 'held off too high and the undercarriage collapsed at contact'.

Brian Considine's first flight was also inauspicious. Born in January 1920, he had attended Ampleforth College in Yorkshire where his exam results were less than exciting, though he did play in the first cricket eleven.

When he left at sixteen, his Housemaster's internal comment on him was 'Strong-willed but hard to guide. Inclined to be resentful of authority. Impetuous and heedless. A certain charm of manner.' He joined Unilever as a trainee executive and when he was nineteen enlisted in the RAFVR in order to learn to fly, completing his elementary training at Gravesend just before the war began. Afterwards he attended No.3 FTS at Grantham, though progress was slow owing to the harsh winter of 1939 and it was not until 10 May – the day that Hitler's forces invaded the Low Countries – that he completed the course. He was then commissioned and a few days later posted to 238 Squadron, following John Wigglesworth who had been on the same course. Neither of them had any operational training whatsoever.

After the old-fashioned biplanes on which he had trained, Considine found the Spitfire 'heavenly'. Unfortunately, on his maiden flight he forgot to change from fine pitch to course pitch once he had reached a certain height, and after one or two circuits he landed, silently congratulating himself on a job well done, when he suddenly saw the CO hopping mad and pointing to the aircraft which was covered in oil. By then Baines was probably running out of paperwork to inflict on his errant pilots.

Meanwhile, a brief moment of excitement was provided on the night of 3 June when 'a 5th Columnist attempted to enter one of this squadron's aircraft at the Dispersal Point. The guard opened fire but the intruder made off.' Accidents were also not the sole preserve of pilots, as Corporal Baird demonstrated on the 7th when he fell from a lifting beam in the hangar whilst engaged on maintenance work. He broke bones in both wrists.

This was the squadron that Sgt Eric Seabourne joined later that month. After only seven hours' flying time in a Hurricane and without ever having fired his guns, he was made operational.

*

Bann's second letter appears to have been written at about this time. It is undated and tells of his escape from France with the British Expeditionary Force (BEF). The letter seems to be the only existing record of the event.

[Letter 2]

Sergeants' Mess,
RAF Station,
Tangmere,
Sussex.
[June? 1940]

Well, Mother and Father, I'm back with the BEF, London, Saturday night, one of the lucky ones. What a scene on Euston Station – never seen anything like it. Crowds gave we boys a wonderful welcome. I managed to get May to come down – my word, what a grand reunion and weekend. We both enjoyed ourselves. I only wish we could have come up to Macclesfield to pay you a visit. I have actually been back three days, but was given an instructional course before being released.

Never in my life have I witnessed such wonderful spirit as shown by the British boys. Thank God, although I could not be so brave myself, that I am British. Orders regular were coming through for all: 'Fight on until you drop, then get up and fight'. That order has been carried out to a man.

All the boys were arriving in London, Saturday night, still wet after swimming to the rescue boats. Mothers, Fathers, Wives, Sweethearts were all waiting there. Some poor devils just stood looking dazed when they realised that their man had paid the price, their faces almost haunted.

Well Father, tell the boys at 'Fairies'[22] not to grumble about all the extra work. We need all your help. All the boys are now anxiously waiting to get fresh planes and get over there to try and save those wonderful boys who remained solid whilst the rest were got aboard for old England. We have been flying this afternoon, not much wasted time, but to see those remaining boys' faces full of hope for our return, even sleep and food do not interest.

Thank you very much for the parcel and letter. Nice to have clean clothes, though May has now come to my help – money, clothes, food, she was grand. But I had lost all, not a thing; I even had to borrow a cigarette from a stranger.

All the boys were the same, but old England was very kind, for cigarettes were dished out at Euston.

Please thank Uncle Tom for the very kind thought. I'm afraid I can't write, but please thank him. I like to write home and to May, but am afraid all the other kind people will have to wait for the time being.

How about the bill for those wedding presents? I do hope, Mother, you managed to fix this up, specially for Winnie. May told me that you had sent me a parcel to Warmwell. So had she, but I am afraid they were lost. Still May has bought me all new underclothes so all's well again.

Met Jack Bann,[23] home from the BEF in London. It's a small world. Please ask Father to ask Fred Johnson if the Cheshire boys are home. We covered a bombing attack upon them, therefore should be very interested to hear if they are safe.

No, the Daily Paper photograph is not me, rather swanking. But I am not a coming pilot – I am almost a veteran, having taken part in squadron operations throughout the whole of the heavy actions.

Cheerio for now, all my kind regards to all in Macclesfield.

To you at home, may I wish you all good health and luck. When I come back again for a rest I might be more lucky and visit home.

Your loving Son
Eric

There is some mystery as to how he came to be stranded in France at this time. His brother believed that he was shot down, though the introduction to the Macclesfield booklet stated that 'his squadron was forced to retreat after their airfield came under attack from advancing German forces. Bann, unable to find a serviceable aircraft that was fit to fly to England, returned via the beaches of Dunkirk with others of his squadron.'

What squadron that was is a moot point. In April, his local newspaper reported that Bann was attached to No. 6 Fighter Squadron; perhaps drawing on this, the Macclesfield booklet stated that he 'was posted to No. 6 Squadron in France'. However, this squadron was not involved in either the Battle of France or the Battle of Britain as it was based abroad throughout that period, and there is no evidence that he was ever part of it. Perhaps there was confusion with his actual posting to No. 6 Flying Training School.

Some writers feel that the letter belongs to the period when Bann was with 253 Squadron, and we know from Guy Harris's letter that pilots were being left to find their own way home. Against this is the fact that Bann tells us that he arrived back on 'Saturday night' and the only Saturday he was with 253 was 18 May, the day he arrived. It is unlikely that he would have been thrust straight into action and Guy Harris, who led 'A' Flight on that day, was convinced that they had never met. John Greenwood, who was with the Flight based in France, also had no memory of him.

The address points to the fact that Bann had by then joined 238 Squadron, and other internal evidence suggests that the letter is later than the first: his clothes have been replaced; the main evacuation of the BEF from Dunkirk took place from 30 May to 4 June (though other ports remained free until later that month); he now considered himself 'almost a veteran'. Moreover, the Cheshire Regiment, to which reference is made, did not evacuate until 1 June. (Some of its members were killed by SS troops in the notorious Wormhoudt massacre on 28 May 1940.) No. 253 Squadron had already ceased operations and 238 did not begin them until 2 July, though in the interim it is evident from Marsh's diary that pilots could be called upon at short notice for duty in France.

The letter tells us that at some stage he was based at RAF Warmwell, a grass airfield just outside Weymouth, for parcels were sent to him there. This group 10 sector airfield in Dorset was the main satellite of Middle Wallop, though 238 Squadron did not move to Middle Wallop until 20 June and did not start using Warmwell until 12 July. Records of the time can be sketchy – the ORB of 253 Squadron, for example, makes no mention of Bann; that of 238 noted his arrival on 21 May but did not mention him again until 2 July when he made one of the first operational sorties. There were no entries at all for the Saturdays 1 and 8 June 1940, which are possible dates for the Saturday referred to. Even Bann's mother seemed to have lost track of him. On 6 June, the *Macclesfield Courier* published an extract from a letter by her that appeared in a section headed 'Serving

Their Country'. She wrote: 'I presume he is now taking part in attacking the enemy, flying a Spitfire machine, so I can only listen to the wireless to hear where these machines are.' His brother Maurice wrote to the author: 'I'm pretty certain that Eric wrote to my Mother and the correct address was deleted and "Somewhere in France" substituted.'[24]

*

By 10 June the war situation was bad enough 'to make the mighty British Empire pretty worried about its existence', according to Marsh's diary. He went on:

> The German army is but a few miles from Paris, having cleared the BEF off the continent. Italy has opened up against us. Bombing has started against England. But the RAF seems to be getting the upper hand. We are hopelessly outnumbered in the air, but better than any two of them.

He was still feeling isolated: 'There are seven sergeants with us,' he wrote, 'all VRs and I don't like 'em.' Having the only car at this time he was much in demand, but even off base he was inclined to keep his distance: 'The sergeants drink two pints then start singing dirty songs,' he recorded. 'They are loud-mouthed and let everyone know they are heroes of the air. The Pilot Officers are too young and easily drunk. In fact the outfit's a wash-out.' It took a visit by Andy to lift his mood and they spent two 'very talkative, happy days' at Brighton and 'drank a few too!' 'What a grand lad he is,' Marsh added. It was criminal to break us up!'

On 11 June, Hurricanes began arriving to replace 238's Spitfires and Gordon Batt had a personal insignia painted on the nose panel of one that he regularly flew – that of a bat flying through a moon. In a snippet from an uncollected letter quoted in the *Macclesfield Times*, Bann wrote: 'We have been given brand new Hurricanes and are determined to leave a clear sky wherever we go. I suppose the time has come now when all of us will have to face the greatest fight of our lives.'[25] Familiarisation flying started all over again, and special duties were allocated to some of the officers, with Urwin-Mann, MacCaw and Firminger being placed in charge of maps, armaments and parachutes respectively. Teething problems persisted, however, and by 15 June were becoming more marked 'owing to the absence of [an] Intelligence Officer and lack of wireless personnel. Equipment and tools still sparse.' [26] That day an advance party left for Middle Wallop, a large grass airfield in Hampshire under the command of W/C David Roberts who later flew occasional sorties with 238.

A Hurricane of 238 Squadron and an unidentified pilot (possibly 'Tony' Marsh)

Ten of their Hurricanes were flown in and F/Lt Kennedy promptly crashed one of them in making a forced landing after running out of petrol. On 18 June, P/O A. R. Wills arrived to act as Intelligence Officer, thus alleviating some of their problems. On the 20th the rest of the squadron relocated to Hampshire, the personnel in very good spirits being transported in four charabancs from which they 'cheered all the girls on the way including their grandmothers'.[27] Everywhere they received the 'thumbs up' in return. Another distraction was provided by an airman on a motor cycle who tried to overtake the charabancs on a hill and ran into a bank when his brakes failed. The squadron was 'much refreshed' by this display.

3
The Deep End
(21 June–13 August 1940)

Marsh found Middle Wallop 'fairly habitable' and becoming 'more so every day'. Their move coincided with the breakthrough of the Germans towards Paris and the Fall of France. For once Marsh was elated. 'Now we're on our own and any spoils or honour we don't share with any half-hearted ally.'[28] From then on, weather permitting, the pilots practised their flying skills, with mixed results. On the day they arrived, Sgt Gardiner crashed for the second time whilst landing at Duxford when his starboard wheel came adrift. Next day, not to be outdone, Marsh crashed again, causing 'slight damage to aileron and one wing tip'. Despite these accidents, the full squadron took to the air in formation for the first time on 26 June. The following night the aerodrome came under attack from an enemy bomber, and thereafter air-raid warnings during the night were frequent.

Marsh recorded their reaction to this 'first taste of war':

> We had previously said that if the air-raid siren went we would just go on sleeping. Such heroic attitude held good on that first night but the next night Jerry spotted our flight-path kindly lit for his guidance by our stupid 'ops' and let go his whistling bombs. Their eerie shriek woke us and we vied with its originator in speed of evacuation of our room. Down in the shelter like Hell-chased hares we had to meet the derisive grins of the wise-heads already down there.[29]

The CO obviously felt that some recreational facilities were needed and bought equipment for rounders and net quoits.

On 2 July the squadron was declared operational and flew fifteen sorties. It had been divided into four sections (Red, Green, Yellow and Blue), each with three aircraft, and their first operational flight fell to Green Section when Urwin-Mann, Firminger and Parkinson took off at 5.36 a.m. to patrol Reading. The final sorties were made after 8 o'clock that evening when Yellow Section (Wigglesworth, Bann and Marsh) patrolled Ringwood. The weather was fine and clear, but nothing was seen all day and no interceptions were made. Everyone was in high spirits and even Marsh seemed revitalised:

> I feel quite a zest for fighting, almost a patriotism – but not quite. I do resent the general attitude to go away on leave or when 'released'. Somehow I want to be in it all the time. Too terribly school-boyish and young but there it is... Somehow I am quite enthusiastic to be the first to bring one down.[30]

The following day, Red Section (Baines, Kennedy and Batt) engaged and chased a Ju 88 and came under fire themselves for the first time. Kennedy's Hurricane was hit and damaged, with bullets penetrating near to the pilot's seat and into the radiator system. On 5 July the squadron suffered its first loss when P/O Firminger flew into Pennings Hill, near Tidworth, in low cloud, and was killed instantly. Six days later, on Thursday, 11 July, the squadron recorded its 'first confirmed scalp'.

At 11.40 a.m., with the Battle of Britain barely a day old, 'B' Flight led by Stuart Walch had taken off to patrol Warmwell in fine weather with good visibility. It comprised Blue Section (Walch, Considine and Little) and

Green Section (Urwin-Mann, MacCaw and Parkinson). At 11.55 they were vectored to Portland which was under attack. As they approached, Walch saw one Me 110 diving towards a ship off Portland Bill and ordered Green Section to remain above in case of escorting fighters. Then with the remainder of Blue Section he swept down to intervene.

All three attacked in order before the hostile aircraft turned towards Walch and he fired several short bursts from about 200-300 yards. Little then engaged again before Walch closed to 50 yards and finished it off. With white and black smoke billowing from its engine, the plane finally plummeted into the sea. Each of them was credited with a third of the 'kill'. This triumph was swiftly followed by a second, for Green Section then pounced on another Me 110 which left the scene in some distress, pursued by Sgt Parkinson although he was out of ammunition. The following day the squadron learned that this aircraft had fallen near to Blandford Forum, 238's second scalp.

The kudos of the squadron's first 'kill' might easily have fallen to Bann some days earlier, as his third letter recounts. Again undated, it describes the events of Sunday, 7 July 1940 and was written on the following Tuesday, the day before the official start of the Battle of Britain. It tells of a sortie with his fellow sergeants Tony Marsh and Gordon Batt (who were flying as a section for the first time) and again illustrates how scanty some of the entries in the ORB can be. For this day the relevant part of the record book reads:

> 15 sorties (being 5 flights of 3 A/C) to do various patrols. About 0900 hrs. A/C thought to be Ju 88 sighted but evaded battle by taking cloud cover before it could be caught.

The record headed Detail of Work Carried Out is even briefer: 'Planes seen and thought to be Ju 88s but not definite. No interception.' Yellow Section had no such doubts as to the number or identity of the aircraft concerned, nor of the interception that followed. No combat reports exist, and the outcome as described in the letter was inconclusive. However, in an account of a dogfight a week later in which Bann claimed a victory, the *Macclesfield Courier* reported: 'On a previous occasion he followed a Junkers 88 for over 100 miles before he managed to shoot it down.'[31] Perhaps he made 238's first 'kill' after all.

[Letter 3]

Sergeants' Mess,
RAF Station,
Middle Wallop,
Hants.
Tuesday.
[9 July 1940]

My Dear Mother and Father,

Thank you both for the nice letters and also the postal order. I was very pleased to hear from Father. Chatty news about things and people I knew so well always provides interest.

I've been having plenty of fun just lately, plenty of anxious moments waiting for the word go, and then plenty of action when up there. I had a most peculiar coincidence this weekend, for whilst out on patrol early Sunday morning my section bumped right into Ju 88s. We just marked a man each. I myself chased my man from Portsmouth up to Bristol. All the way up he kept me at bay by means of his cannon firing to the rear. However, we had a chase through the clouds over Bristol and then he foxed me by cutting his engine and I went sailing right under him.

A very anxious moment followed whilst I got off his tail. Eventually he turned tail for the coast and I was after him with everything that I had got, the engine flat out with my emergency pulled flat out. I thought my ears were going to burst, for we were diving from 25,000 feet. Well, I didn't see him come down, though all his guns were out of action. When I arrived back at our base, the other two were still going at it. Eventually Gordon Batt came down at Rissington and I asked the CO if I could go up in Batt's car to see if he was OK.[32] I found him fine, though his machine was being repaired. Before leaving Wallop I was told that we were free for 24 hours and so we continued on to Birmingham for Sunday evening. They were very surprised to see me and very pleased.

Well, that is enough about myself. How are all of you at home? I think our work has prevented many of the invading planes reaching and spoiling your night's rest. I hope so anyhow. Bye-the-bye, ask Father to please thank Fred Johnson for his very kind letter, though I will make time eventually to write and thank him myself. I enjoyed his news about all the boys. I often wonder how the local 'Terriers' are getting along.

Mother, we three Sergeants have formed a section, 'Yellow', and I want to know if you could get us three silk yellow scarves or squares, and bye-the-bye, I would very much like to pay my debts, so please make out your bill and send same along.

Have you found any cheap motor bikes, Father? We are hoping to run them for next to nothing – petrol and oil free, and plenty of mechanics to carry out repairs.

Ah well, cheerio for now. All my kind regards to the good people in Macclesfield.

Your loving Son
Eric

The scarves that he requested for the three of them were duly purchased and sent down to him. Their section usually flew one of the most vulnerable positions as it tried to protect the rear and its members were called 'arse-end Charlies'. This might have created a special bond, but for Marsh there was never any possibility of this new trio of sergeants replacing the old one. 'They've made Yellow Section an all-sergeant affair,' he noted in his diary. 'Batt and Bann are with me now. If anything that's a disadvantage. Both are keen enough but so young and thoughtless. I have to be quite firm with them at times.'[33] In their free time Bann preferred to be with his wife whenever he could, and although the other two socialised they seldom developed the kind of easy relationship that Marsh had enjoyed with Andy and Mac. Together they had recently visited Bournemouth and Coventry, though the former had been 'spoilt by the attitude of our young friend Batt', while the latter 'was again marred by his stupidity'. Marsh goes on: 'But I met a rather interesting girl there – so he's forgiven and she's forgotten.'

However, tensions began to simmer and later that month he and Batt went to Ruislip in an endeavour to clear the air for the sake of the section. Any harmony that was established seemed transitory, however, for after the action described in the following letter Batt indirectly accused Marsh of 'standing out of the fight' and leaving all the work to him. 'Poor Batt,' Marsh wrote at what seemed a new low in their relationship.

*

On 12 July, a party of 25 men and NCOs went to Warmwell to prepare for the refuelling and rearming of the aircraft of 238 and 601 Squadrons, both of which were to use it as a forward base during daytime. No. 238's pilots were very much the poor relations, for 601, led by the Honourable Max Aitken, son of Lord Beaverbrook, was not nicknamed 'the Millionaires' Squadron' for nothing. Gordon Batt noted that their greatcoats and uniforms were lined with red silk, and stories of their conspicuous wealth abounded. One officer, detailed to solve a temporary petrol shortage, went off with his cheque book and bought a local filling station.

Bann's fourth (undated) letter is headed 'September 1940' in the Macclesfield booklet but was in fact written on Sunday, 14 July, and describes the events of the previous day. That Saturday, the Squadron flew 38 sorties totalling 21½ hours' flying and claimed two Me 110s and a Dornier in the Weymouth locality. The successful engagements occurred during the afternoon when Blue Section (Walch, Considine and Seabourne) made the first kill in an assault on 20-plus Me 110s circling over Portland Bill. Walch attacked one before Considine fired several short bursts into the following aircraft and saw flames spurt from its port engine. It dived vertically down but Considine could not watch it hit the sea as he had another Me 110 on his tail. He spun away and broke off the engagement as his reflector sight had failed.

Bann, flying with Marsh and Batt, gave details in his combat report of their interception in the same area, during which he destroyed one of the German planes:

> In line astern formation when ordered to tackle individually. Got inside Me 110 and detached it from formation and made quarter attack. One 2-

106

second burst, he immediately dived into sea and with line astern attack he went straight in.

Saw 1 Dornier 17 with port engine on fire losing height very rapidly. Believed due to 'B' Flight, Green Section, same squadron. (*Handwritten addition to the typed report*) LATER. Confirmed that this had been shot down by Yellow Section, 609 Squadron.

His reference to the Dornier illustrates the difficulties in verifying claims. He is sometimes credited with a third of this 'kill', though it is clear that he was not involved. He believed that it was a scalp for 238's Green Section (Urwin-Mann, MacCaw and Seabourne), although the ORB attributed it to Red Section (Kennedy, Davis and Parkinson). Combat reports describe how Kennedy made the initial attack before the other two both fired on the plane and saw it crash into the sea off Chesil Beach. However, the later note (presumably added by the Intelligence Officer) ascribed the 'kill' to another section of an altogether different squadron.

After this engagement, F/Lt Kennedy – 'an officer of high calibre' – was lost. During the attack on the lone Dornier, he was bounced by three Messerschmitts and his Hurricane damaged. Kennedy made a desperate attempt to crash-land but his plane stalled as he tried to avoid high tension cables and he was killed, the first Australian to die in the Battle of Britain. On the day the letter was written, the BBC broadcast the extraordinary commentary that Charles Gardner had recorded of the dogfight as it was taking place. Many Macclesfield citizens were listening and thrilled to the blow-by-blow account. Bann's mother was one, though she had no idea that her son was involved until she received his letter.

Middle Wallop.
Sunday.
[14 July 1940]

Dear Mother and Father,

First let me thank all of you for your very kind letters. Thank Maurice also for his letter and again thanks for your photograph.

Now, let me tell you of my greatest and most exciting air battle. Yesterday six of us ran into 25 fighters (German) – there was a grand account given by the BBC. However, my first thought was 'Here goes – I'll fight', but four of them each made things just too bad. Well, I ducked and fought like a madman – I am sure at those moments one is not normal. I looked up once and the air was full of machines and lead all milling round for that final burst. Well, here I am, not touched, thank God, and have one fighter to my credit. We drove every one away and got the warmest praise from all. Unfortunately for us, we lost our Flight Commander, poor fellow, engaged to a charming girl three weeks ago. I am afraid he never had a chance, three of Germany's best planes right on his tail, and we too busy to help.

Such are the fortunes of war. And now, how's everyone? Still going hard at it, I suppose. Oh, by-the-bye, don't bother doing anything about my car. We really only wanted the motor bikes to dash about the aerodrome. Not going to tax, however. I don't intend to pay a lot for that job.

And now, cheerio for now, short but sweet, but letting you know that I am still living.

Eric

Eric Bann in 1940

*

On the day Kennedy died, F/Lt Donald Turner and P/O William Towers-Perkins joined the squadron. Don Turner had been born in Port Stanley in the Falkland Islands in 1910, but was educated in England. After service as a territorial in the Artists Rifles, he joined the RAF on a short service commission in 1932 and served with several squadrons before the outbreak of war. He brought more welcome experience to the squadron, becoming its 'A' Flight Commander. Towers-Perkins was educated at the Cardinal Vaughan School and Queen Mary College, London, learning to fly as a member of the University Air Squadron. He was called up in November 1939 and commissioned. After further training he was posted to 238 Squadron, though he had to undergo a conversion course to fly Hurricanes before he was ready for action.

They were followed the day after by 31-year-old Harold Fenton, who took over as Commanding Officer on 15 July.

Born in Argentina, 'Jimmy' Fenton had graduated from Trinity College, Dublin, and then held a short service commission in the RAF from 1928 to 1933, part of which was spent on the North West Frontier. Afterwards he was placed on the Reserve and became a civil flying instructor. On the outbreak of war he was recalled, and although he had only 15 hours' operational training himself, he would prove to be a popular and effective leader.

'Jimmy' Fenton (left) with 'Johnnie' Johnson

He found that his fledgling squadron had been placed on 'readiness' but was anything but ready: 'Most of the others,' he recalled, 'were new from Flying Training Schools...We badly needed even a few days to get to know each other and work out tactics but this was not possible... [We] just had to jump in at the deep end without any unit training whatsoever.'[34] Brian Considine remembered that the squadron was still flying the old-fashioned Vic formation of three aircraft which may have been impressive in pre-war air displays but could be suicidal in air combat. It is hardly surprising that during the Battle of Britain, when it was often at the forefront of the action, the squadron would pay a terrible price. Seventeen of its pilots were killed, the second highest casualty rate of any fighter squadron.[35]

There followed several days of poor weather with little of note happening. Gordon Batt in his war memoir evoked a typical day of this period, with its mixture of waiting, boredom, lurking tension and then sudden frenetic activity:

> Report to the Flight hut on the airfield half an hour before dawn. We would be allocated an aircraft – we had our own mostly – but servicing upset this sometimes. We would put our parachutes in the cockpit or on the wing, don our Mae Wests, then return to the Nissen hut, which was mainly full of beds, and lie down and wait. If you had no feelings you could sleep!
>
> The main trouble was the phone. This was manned by an Erk [aircraftman], who was our communication link with the controller and all and sundry on the station. So the damn thing would ring for things like permission granted for someone to carry out a test flight, then maybe a time check, change of duties, etc. until you got to the stage when you said 'Sod the thing, I am going to sleep'. Then it would ring again and the Erk would shout: '*Squadron scramble! Angels fifteen Portsmouth.*' He would also run outside and ring a bell, as a signal for the ground crews to start engines.
>
> We would dash out to our aircraft – the engines would burst into life – and as we put on our parachutes the fitter would get out of the cockpit, then stand on the wing ready to help strap us in after we had donned our helmets which had been draped

over the control column, then we waved chocks away and moved off...It was a glorious sight to see twelve aircraft taking off, although I must confess that I always felt vulnerable until I had the wheels up and the cockpit hood closed.

We did not always make contact with the enemy. Sometimes they would veer away and attack further east, or just push off. When we did make contact, the CO would radio '*Tally-ho*'. That was the time to turn the firing button to fire, then wait for the CO to put us into a position to attack...We were usually outnumbered by four to one – in a way this was not a bad thing as we had more targets than they did.[36]

Unsurprisingly, the telephone became so abhorred that many survivors of the Battle of Britain vowed never to have one in their homes.

On 18 July, Sgt Leslie Pidd joined the squadron and was soon in action with both Blue and Yellow Sections. The 21-year-old had been born in August 1918 in Patrington, near Hull, the youngest of five children. During the First War his father George Pidd had served in the merchant navy and in 1917 won the Distinguished Service Medal for his part in helping to repel a submarine attack on his ship, the SS *Aracataca*. The family eventually moved to Dunswell, and Leslie attended the village school and then Beverley Grammar School before starting work as a mechanic. In December 1938, he enlisted in the RAFVR and was called up on the outbreak of war, being posted to No. 8 Flying Training School at Montrose in Scotland, from which he graduated on 13 May 1940.

He was then posted to 17 Squadron, which was soon involved in covering the retreat of the BEF from France.

Pidd, though, needed to gain further flying experience and was sent to No. 6 Operational Training Unit [OTU] to convert to Hurricanes before re-joining the squadron, probably in June. He then flew with it until his transfer to 238 came through. In the meantime he had become engaged to his childhood sweetheart from Dunswell, Marjorie Noble, with their wedding planned for that autumn. Like the others, however, his more immediate concern was staying alive.

Leslie Pidd and his fiancée Marjorie

*

On the evening of 19 July, Marsh led Yellow Section on a long convoy patrol and it was dusk when they came in to land. After a drinking session the previous day, Marsh had been feeling queasy and fluffed the landing, breaking the undercarriage:

> I was unhurt but they rushed me into hospital and prescribed a few days' rest though otherwise fit for flying…The CO was quite decent – we have a new one – Baines would have hung me!

113

> That's my third mishap with 238 Squadron (the numbers add up to 13!) so it may have serious consequences. Lord! I don't want to get posted from fighters.[37]

The lull in the fighting ended abruptly on the afternoon of the 20th when 238 was back in the 'deep end', with three sections in action while on convoy patrol. Blue Section (Walch, Pidd and Seabourne) took off just before mid-day, but eventually they all became separated. Just after Walch had turned on his reserve tank and decided to return to base, he saw bombs exploding around one of the convoy's escorting destroyers. He immediately 'pulled the plug'[38] and went after the enemy aircraft which had turned southwards. He then came across three Me 109s and without hesitation dived to attack, opening fire on his chosen target from 200 yards and closing to 50 yards: 'Two 2-second bursts were fired. Black smoke poured from under the engine of the E/A [enemy aircraft] and he turned right and made [a] vertical dive towards the sea.' At once Walch was set upon by the two remaining fighters but managed to escape. Meanwhile, Seabourne had located Pidd and together they followed a third Hurricane until they grew suspicious and turned tail, returning to base. It was later surmised that they had followed a captured Hurricane being flown by a German pilot.

In the second engagement, Red Section (Turner, Davis and Parkinson) was not so lucky when it intercepted six 109s to the south of Swanage. In his combat report Davis related what happened:

> I saw a Hurricane (Red 3 Sgt Parkinson) shot down in flames by an Me 109 and dived on this E/A and fired two or three short bursts of 2 seconds each. My dive was for about 2,000 feet from 14,000 feet

and I made a stern attack. The Me 109 went into a vertical dive but flattened out about 5 feet above sea. I dived down on him again and fired several very long bursts which went into the Me 109 from the stern and it started to burn furiously with clouds of black smoke but I did not see the A/C crash as I was then attacked by two other Me 109s. I broke off the engagement by doing a steep diving turn to the right. The E/A made no attempt to follow me but made straight for home. The enemy shooting was very bad and I had no ammunition left.

Charles Davis

F/Lt Turner was witnessing these events from about 12,000 feet and saw Parkinson bale out into the Channel. Then an Me 109 passed far beneath him. 'I dived on his tail,' he wrote, 'and gave him one short burst at about 100 yards and he immediately dived vertically. I saw him pull out at sea level and followed him down and fired another short burst and he went straight into the sea. I circled round and saw a large patch of oil and a lot of foam but no sign of the aircraft or pilot.'

In the final engagement Green Section (Urwin-Mann, MacCaw and Little) spotted a completely white aircraft seven miles from the convoy. Urwin-Mann went to investigate and identified it as an He 59 seaplane. He dived to attack and put its starboard engine out of action, leaving it dead on the water three miles from the French coast. These successes were tempered by the loss of Parkinson who was eventually picked up by the crew of HMS *Acheron* but died shortly afterwards.[39] It was the squadron's first loss of an NCO pilot – 'one who was of great resource and daring'.

The 21st proved a better day for the squadron. In the morning Red Section (Turner, Davis and Wigglesworth) intercepted an Me 110 ten miles south west of Middle Wallop. In a 'running engagement' all three fired at it as it weaved in and out of clouds, the aircraft adopting 'the most unusual evasive tactics – stall turns, half rolls, etc.' It was last seen with smoke pouring from its starboard engine and was eventually found crashed at Goodwood. The only damage in return was a bullet through Turner's propeller. They added to their score that afternoon when they were joined by Yellow Section (Fenton and Batt) and shot down a Dornier 17 over Blandford, Batt delivering the final strike. This time Davis' plane was damaged but he landed safely. Later still, on convoy patrol at Portland, Blue Section (Walch, Considine and Little) took on 15 Me 110s that were in the act of dive-bombing. Walch made short work of one, while Considine set the starboard engine of another on fire.

Several days of poor visibility followed during which there was little activity. Indeed, the entry in the ORB for the 24th recorded 'No flying. Most unusual.' As soon as they were released, the pilots who were mainly young and single were wont to indulge their chief interests – 'booze and girls'. A favourite watering-hole for Middle Wallop fliers was the Square Club at Andover, where a slim, black-haired girl named 'Terry' (nicknamed 'Gypsy') had an eye for the 'Brylcream Boys'. However, she began to be regarded as 'unlucky' when pilots she had known disappeared suddenly, and some would have nothing to do with her as a result.

The squadron's ranks were swollen by the arrival of F/Lt James McArthur on 22 July and, a week later, by P/O Vernon Simmonds. Meanwhile Marsh and Batt had revisited Coventry where Marsh met Batt's father. They also had 'the rather unpleasant job of visiting Parky's parents. They were pretty cut up.' Then they went drinking and met up with girlfriends. Their uneasy relationship persisted, however, – at least on Marsh's side who found that Batt was 'particularly disgusting' that trip: 'Four of them had shot down a Dornier and he had a souvenir from it. To hear of his yarns the town must have thought that Hitler's Air Force suffered a sad blow.'[40] Marsh was mindful that he was the only one of the section not to have opened his score – indeed he had damaged more of their own aircraft that those of the enemy. Perhaps Batt was indirectly rubbing it in.

When they returned, Marsh, hung-over again, found to his horror that he had been detailed for a spot of night flying practice – an experience that none of the pilots looked forward to. Leslie Pidd had expressed some anxiety in a letter to his brother Stan, who was at the RAF Technical

School at Locking, near Weston-Super-Mare. The latter replied: 'I suppose your game isn't too good at the best of times... Did you go up on Tuesday night? I hope the rain came down in bucketsful so you wouldn't have to... I can quite imagine anyone getting a bit jittery at the prospect of night flying but you can only do one thing kid and that is to keep your chin up.' Marsh was certainly a bit jittery at the prospect. Convinced that this would be the last time he flew a Hurricane, he took off in the half light and made 'a pretty bloody landing'. Nothing was damaged, however, and so the ordeal was on. At first he considered crying off, but then continued and made three good landings, the last in the dark. He was 'vastly relieved and not a little surprised'.

The following day, 25 July, Yellow Section was back in action when the squadron flew 24 sorties, the last twelve to intercept an enemy raid that was said to be approaching the coast, but the ORB recorded that 'not a sausage was seen'. On the 26th, however, shortly after Bann had lost his section in cloud and returned to base, the rest of 'A' and 'B' Flights made contact. After a head-on attack, Sgt Little found part of his boot shot away and two bullets in his parachute. Walch was more successful and with one short burst inflicted terminal damage on an Me 109 which 'half rolled, then dived vertically down, then went into a spin and broke up, the wings dropping off and the fuselage going into the sea.' Meanwhile, Marsh had had a squirt at two 109s with no discernible effect. He later gave this account of the action:

> We were sent off on a 'flap' and we went over to the French (now German) coast to meet 6 Me 109s. Although the squadron were there only F/Lt Walch and myself were fighting. He got his but mine got

away. I wish I'd got one. It would help my case quite a lot. Group are considering my crash now.[41]

*

Bann's fifth letter describes how he too was shot down into the 'drink', an event that happened at about this time. There is some mystery about this episode which went unmentioned in 238's records and in standard reference books. Consequently there has been much speculation regarding the date when the incident occurred. Given the details in the letter ('The CO and two of us were out on early morning patrol...'), it is possible to isolate the two occasions in July when Bann was flying with the CO and one other pilot. The first took place on the 4th when he, Marsh and S/L Baines patrolled Swanage. However, the patrol happened at 9.50 a.m. (hardly 'early morning') and then joined Blue Section. No interception took place, as Marsh recorded in his diary:

> On that trip we flew aimlessly about over Weymouth but saw only the results of the Huns' bombs – one big ship burning and a small boat sinking but Jerry had long since departed. How he must laugh at our fighters! But he won't always.

The second occasion was on 27 July 1940. That day Bann, Davis and S/L Fenton were making early morning sorties to patrol a convoy codenamed 'Bacon' in Weymouth Bay. The first of these began at 4.40 a.m. and passed without incident. On the second sortie, however, starting at 8.33 a.m., they were suddenly in action, as Davis' combat report narrates:

> I was Red 2 but took over leadership for CO at 0930 as his R/T was useless, and saw at 0950 about 12 Ju

119

87s escorted by Me 109s flying at about 13,000 feet. We were at about 9,000. I climbed behind as they turned towards France (position approximately 10 miles south of Swanage) and ordered section to pick E/A. I came astern of extreme left hand Ju 87. They were in no formation. I fired one short burst (approximately 2 seconds) from 250 yards, closing rapidly from astern and saw E/A start to burn (black smoke) from starboard wing. E/A then dropped its bombs at random into the sea. I fired another long burst (about 5 seconds) at 100 yards from astern and saw bits fly off machine and it turned on its back and dived vertically into the sea. Both S/L Fenton and Sgt. Bann (Red 1 and 3) saw this and confirm it.

Afterwards, the ORB tells us, 'S/L Fenton chased [an] Me 109 which was attacking a Hurricane and followed it to two miles off the French coast'. He could not bring it down, and, short of petrol and ammunition, had to abandon the pursuit and land at Warmwell.

These details match some of those of the letter – the time, the area, the odds, the destruction of one bomber and the subsequent pursuit – and the Hurricane under attack may have been Bann's.[42]

[Letter 5]   Middle Wallop,
                                                    Friday.
                                            2 August 1940

Dear Mother and Father,
    At last I have found time to write and thank all of you for the nice letters and grand parcels. I am very sorry for not having written sooner, but things have been impossible just lately.

First let me wish you Mother many happy returns of the day.[43] Trusting that you are well and cheery of spirit. I only wish that I could have managed to make a trip home upon your birthday. It would have been very nice.

Have been having lots of fun just lately. Have been missing for three days.[44] Poor old May's heart was in her mouth but I got 24 hours' leave upon arriving back at the Base just to go and prove to the dear girl that I was really OK.

The CO and two of us were out on early morning patrol when along came a shower of bombers to attack our convoy. In we went, roaring all over the sky, with odds of seven to one, but this time I could not dodge quick enough and I was knocked for six, right into the English Channel. Gosh it was cold so early in the morning! Well I broke all swimming records and was eventually picked up by a boat and landed at Portsmouth. There they detained me just to make sure that I was all right. However, apart from a few gallons of sea water in my stomach I was otherwise OK and I have been doing plenty of flying since. I was also very pleased to find that the other two were OK and had managed to shoot down one bomber and drive the rest home before they even reached the convoy.

How's everyone at home? Please convey my kind regards to all, also in case I don't get a chance to write please thank Miss Warhurst and Auntie Hilda for their nice parcels. I will write to them as soon as I get a few moments to spare.

Cheerio for now. All my kind regards to Father and Maurice, trusting both are keeping well.

Your loving Son
Eric

May's birthday 7 August.

Have 24 hours' leave 5-6 August, noon Monday until noon Tuesday. Do you think any of you could get down to Birmingham – should very much like to see you.

*

Besides fretting over his future as a fighter pilot, Marsh had more mundane concerns on his mind. A planned outing to Stratford with a girlfriend had to be put off when his free day did not materialise. Then there was his financial situation:

> Having expenses lately:
> £6 to Limited Finance
> £5.10 to Taxation Dept.
> £5 to Insurance for car
> £1 Mess bill
> £25 Income Tax
> – and I'm fighting for my country! Funny isn't it!!

It was to be the last entry in his diary.

The first few days of August brought changeable weather with poor visibility and little in the way of action. It was time for some changes to the personnel to be made. F/Lt McArthur was transferred to 609 Squadron as a Flight Commander and F/O Towers-Perkins was attached to 6 OTU for three weeks. On the 4th, twenty-two-year-old F/O David Hughes and nineteen-year-old Sgt Geoffrey Gledhill joined the squadron from that unit, followed the day after by F/O Michal Steborowski and Sgt Marian Domagala, two veteran Polish pilots who were both thirty-one. The arrival of the Poles – and later the Czechs – was, in the words of S/L Fenton, 'like manna from heaven'. Bann became particularly friendly with Domagala, who had been an instructor at the Polish Central Flying School and who often flew in Yellow Section. Gordon Batt put his own survival down to him. Domagala also flew as No. 2 to 'Jimmy' Fenton, the CO, who 'found it reassuring to have a man of his determination and ability on my wingtip'.[45]

Marian Domagala

Bann's admiration for another of the squadron's pilots, Don Turner, found expression in a snippet from a second uncollected letter quoted in the *Macclesfield Times*. Describing an encounter over the Channel in which he was one of six pilots who confronted 80 Messerschmitts and Junkers, he wrote: 'Our Flight Commander is absolutely fearless and he led us through what seemed to me to be the impossible. Well, Mother and Father, though terribly tired I am, touch wood, without a scratch.'[46]

His sixth letter is again headed 'September 1940' in the Macclesfield booklet but was written on Sunday 11 August 1940, and refers initially to the events of the preceding Thursday, 8 August. That day the squadron was at readiness at first light and scrambled repeatedly. At 12.09 it took off to intercept a raid of 40 aircraft on the 'Peewit' convoy, about six miles south of the Needles. The protective balloon barrage had already been shot down and enemy aircraft were dive-bombing the convoy when 238 arrived. A confused swirling dogfight then ensued, during which nine 'kills' were claimed, with four confirmed. (The tally in the letter is over-optimistic.) The newcomer Steborowski was flying as part of Blue Section with Walch and Little when they spotted enemy aircraft 8,000 feet below them. He followed Walch down but when he pulled out of the dive he momentarily blacked out. When he recovered he saw an Me 110 and latched onto its tail, seeing tracer coming at him from the rear gunner. Steborowski closed before opening fire himself: 'I began to fire at about 250 yards from astern (about 5 short bursts of 2–3 seconds each) and I saw the bullets go into the E/A. I think the first burst killed the rear gunner as I received no rear fire. After this the E/A turned right and left very slowly and went down into a dive.' His 'kill' was one of those unconfirmed.

Gordon Batt, flying as Yellow 3, saw an Me 109 on a Hurricane's tail and as the Hurricane did a left-hand climbing turn with the 109 in pursuit, Batt got inside the turn and fired two quarter deflection bursts of about two-seconds each. The enemy aircraft flew into the bullets and Batt saw it stall turn and then dive steeply downwards. Almost immediately he glimpsed another 109 in his rear-view mirror and broke sharply away. As he had not witnessed the outcome, he too had to be satisfied with 'one unconfirmed'.

The successes were credited to Davis and Hughes (Me 110s) and Seabourne and Domagala (Me 109s). Seabourne had seen two 109s pass about 100 feet above his cockpit though they made no attempt to attack. Then he saw a third behind the others making a shallow climbing turn to the left. His combat report records the 'kill' that followed:

> I climbed inside him and gave short (3 second burst) from about 75 yards quarter deflection right into his cockpit. He rolled over on his back and dived down and I got on his tail and followed him down, giving another 3-second burst from astern at about 100 yards. I followed him to 10,000 feet and circled, watching his descent. He just hit the sea and exploded, going in absolutely vertically.

The four clear victories, however, had come at a price. After the scrap, section leader Derek MacCaw and the 'A' Flight Commander Don Turner were both posted 'missing' and never found. Turner was believed to have baled out and, as there was no rescue launch in the area, S/L Fenton decided to look for him – on his own as all the other aircraft were being refuelled. When he reached the site he discovered a German seaplane which he attacked, but in return was hit by a lucky shot that cut an oil pipe. Soon afterwards his engine seized and he ditched close to the Admiralty Armed Trawler HMS *Basset*, injuring his head and chest in the process. He was fished out and put in the boiler room, taking tea and toast there with a German pilot who was rescued soon afterwards. This was *Oberleutnant* Martin Müller whose total possessions were a Very pistol and cartridges and twelve condoms! They were both transferred to the Haslar hospital where Fenton received 17 stitches to his forehead and several visits from anxious pilots of 238. He was then given three weeks' sick leave. Müller spent five chaste years in captivity.

The ORB paid tribute to two more lost pilots:

> F/O MacCaw came to the RAF through the University of Cambridge and had been with an Army Co-op. Squadron before coming to 238, of which he was an original pilot. Of Celtic colouring – blue eyes and black hair, which was already tinged with grey – his slightly dreamy, dignified personality is greatly missed. He was clearly material from which the best type of officer is made.
>
> F/Lt Turner's keenness, energy and good humour made him very popular with everyone, and his strong reliable character made him an excellent second-in-command. He has been greatly missed.

Bann goes on to refer to a 'further great fight' that day from which he had just returned. On 11 August, at 10.35 a.m., twelve sorties comprising 'A' and 'B' Flights had met a force of 150 plus bandits (or 'sky rats' as the ORB frequently calls them), some of which were dive-bombing the Portland area where fires could be seen. The two flights joined battle in separate places – 'A' Flight (of which Bann was a member) two miles east of Weymouth and 'B' Flight five miles south of Swanage. The squadron had 4 victories confirmed, with Marsh finally claiming a 'kill', though he had to share it with Bann. Marsh began the assault, as he related in his combat report:

> I saw an He 111 about 200 yards away from the other E/A and attacked. I fired 8 one-second bursts from about 300 yards, closing to nil, at slightly above and from astern, the last burst I fired was about 4 seconds. The port engine was smoking and E/A started to turn to port. Yellow 2 continued the attack and I took [on] three escorting fighters. I was not able to see the He 111 go into the sea. I was then

involved with the three 109s and used evasive tactics and eventually dived into the cloud owing to damaged starboard aileron from the He 111 rear gunner. Landed at Middle Wallop on orders from Controller 1135. Number of rounds fired 400.

With Marsh otherwise engaged, it was left to Bann to deliver the *coup de grâce:*

> I made number two attack and fired a fairly long burst of about 3 seconds from 150 yards, closing in a vertical attack. The E/A exploded and fell into the water. I found two Me 109s on my tail and broke away and did a steep turn to evade them. After that I found myself outnumbered and it took all my time doing evasive tactics. I eventually gained height and proceeded towards Portland and patrolled as ordered and eventually was ordered to land. Landed at Middle Wallop 1135. No. of rounds fired, 480.

In the turmoil of the dogfight, Domagala was finishing off an Me 109 when a Hurricane flew between them and was also shot down by some of his bullets. It was not known what squadron the aircraft came from but the pilot was believed to have baled out. Their own casualties were catastrophic. The whole of Blue Section (Walch, Steborowski and Gledhill) was lost in a hail of fire from an overwhelming number of enemy fighters, while Frederick Cawse of Green Section was also shot down and killed. Any satisfaction on the part of the German pilot was short-lived, for Urwin-Mann (Green 1) had witnessed the event and in turn destroyed the Me 109. Meanwhile, Sgt Pidd of the same section was fighting to survive in his badly damaged Hurricane that was still under periodic attack:

> I sustained a heavy burst of machine-gun and shell-gun fire which shot practically all starboard rudder

away, caused considerable damage to starboard wing and I received also numerous other perforations and damage to engine, including glycol feed, and liquid gushed into cockpit. I pulled into a steep turn and got inside one E/A and fired a quarter deflection shot at about 300 yards (2-second burst) and I could see tracer going straight along the fuselage and cockpit. The E/A immediately went over into a left-hand spin and disappeared from my vision, spinning continuously down vertically. I did not see it hit the sea but it appeared to be out of control. I made straight for the shore owing to the damaged condition of A/C but was later attacked near coast by a single Me 109 at which I was able to fire a very short one-second burst deflection at about 2,000 yards in order to scare him away, as my engine was smoking. The aircraft was almost uncontrollable and the cockpit full of oil and smoke.

This E/A turned to right and dived down, and I fell into a spin straight after that. I lost 7,000 feet in recovery but eventually landed at Warmwell.

There he sustained his only injury – a cut to his hand as he was alighting from his machine. Of 'B' Flight, only Urwin-Mann managed to get back to base.

The ORB's tributes are again worthy of note:

F/Lt Walch was an officer of very great promise. He was dauntless in the face of danger, careless of his own personal safety and comfort, thoughtful for all who came in contact with him, and had an innate gift for administrative duty which should have taken him high in his country's service. A Tasmanian, he had been in the Royal Australian Air Force and had come to this country about 3 years ago to join the RAF, and was one of the original Flight Commanders of this squadron.

F/O Steborowski was a Polish Officer Pilot of great experience who had been with the squadron but a short time. He had flown in Poland and was of a very cheerful nature – his rugged face and gentle smile are greatly missed. He is the first Pole to be lost by this squadron.

P/O Cawse had also been but a short time in the squadron.[47] A man of quiet manner and a happy disposition, he should have been most useful. (*Remainder illegible*)

Sgt Gledhill had been in the squadron barely a week and had hardly time to get to know his comrades or they to know him. A gentle boy, ruddy of countenance – he is the second NCO pilot to be lost. He went down in his first engagement with the enemy. This day four Hurricanes were lost. The only reflection of good there is in a gloomy day is the thought that these gentlemen of England have exacted a toll which will go far to wear down the German Beast.

Frederick Norman Cawse

Both Walch and Cawse had known 'Gypsy' from the Square Club; indeed Walch had been out with her the previous night and had not returned to base until the early hours of that day. Now both of them had been lost on the same sortie. Perhaps the pilots' superstitions were not entirely baseless.

As a result of these devastating losses of some of 238's most experienced and senior pilots, F/O Hughes, who had been with the squadron for only a week, found himself acting as its CO on 12 August.

[Letter 6]

Middle Wallop,
Sunday.
[11 August 1940]

Dear Mother, Father and 'Sandy',

Thanks very much for the letter. Very sorry for not having written sooner, but I have been going great guns.

Have been having a real hectic week, the invasion having started in real earnest. Have been right in the thick of it. Our Squadron managed to bag 21 planes on Thursday. Never in all my life have I had such a flying day and never before have I seen so many planes. However, yours truly managed again to come out OK, thank God. However, we lost our Flight Commander and Section leader, poor fellows, then followed our Commanding Officer, and today I have just come back from a further great fight. I think our report in the news tomorrow will even better Thursday's record. But we were again first there and consequently suffered our losses. Only one pilot returned from 'B' Flight, so we now have only pilots without CO or Flight Commander. I think they will have to make me a Squadron Leader. I am pleased to say that my 'bag' keeps going up.

Have made great friends with a young Pole Air Force pilot, two having joined our squadron. His tale of how the Germans machine-gunned all his people and his life hunted by the 'Gestapo' police before he eventually managed to escape to England, well it just made my blood boil. He does not want to live, only seek revenge upon the Germans who have killed and taken all that matters in life. Poland, he states, is just hell, its people and food ravaged by bloodthirsty men of the 'Gestapo'.

My leave has gone for six, even my 24 hours today has gone. Still, never mind. May God help keep me alive and I'll be with you all one of these fine days, so don't worry or be disappointed with this cruel news.

All my kind regards to you all,
Eric

*

Combat fatigue had been taking its toll for some time and the squadron was reaching the point of burn-out. Thankfully, 12 August provided a welcome break in the action. Sgt Pidd, whose 22nd birthday it was, was back in the air with the rest of the squadron on patrol over Bembridge and Portland but nothing was seen. Later that afternoon they were dispatched to Warmwell to investigate suspicious aircraft which turned out to be Blenheims. The same day the Adjutant, F/O A. N. David, flew to Colerne for a meeting with Air Vice-Marshal Sir Quintin Brand (Air Officer Commanding No.10 Fighter Group under whose control the squadron had passed a few days earlier) and Air Commodore John Cole-Hamilton. It was decided that the squadron should withdraw from the front line and relocate to St Eval on 14 August.

Before that it had to endure one more gruelling day of action – *Adlertag* (Eagle Day). On Tuesday 13 August, many sorties were flown, with Bann, Considine and Wigglesworth on patrol at 6 a.m. when they caught sight of about 30 Me 110s that immediately turned tail and fled. Shortly afterwards, to the south of the Isle of Wight, nine members of the squadron were surprised from above by a large formation of Me 109s and 110s. In the nick of time Urwin-Mann spotted them and shouted a warning. Sgt Seabourne made an audacious attack on three of them, destroying two before being shot up by the third. With his aircraft ablaze, he could feel the rubber goggles melting on his face and tried to bale out, but his cockpit hood was jammed. He was still under attack when a wing broke off and his Hurricane lurched over, hurling him through the hood and allowing him to fall free. After floating in the Channel for an age, he was picked up by the destroyer HMS *Bulldog* and filled with morphine. He was later hospitalised at Portsmouth with severe burns and a broken leg sustained during his rescue.

As Gordon Batt was going in to attack he suddenly felt as if his Hurricane had been hit by a steamroller. With his engine dead, his prop motionless and his 'oil tank shot about', he knew he had to get down quickly and made a forced landing, wheels up, in a field of barley. In a flash he unbuckled, ran along the wing and then fell head first into the barley. When he got up, he saw the Home Guard advancing with rifles at the ready and, covered in oil and barley, he thought it prudent to raise his hands in the air. Once his identity was established he was conveyed to Tangmere where he tried to clean himself up in the toilets. As he left, the Station Warrant Officer roared at him, 'Sergeant, where's your hat?' and was left open-mouthed by Batt's robust response.

At 11.55 a.m. eleven members of the squadron took off to patrol Portland where they confronted a mixed formation of 50 plus bandits. Yellow Section (Marsh, Domagala and Bann) climbed into the sun and Marsh delivered an attack against an Me 110 that had become slightly separated. After he had fired one burst of about four seconds, the port engine of the enemy aircraft started smoking and the pilot baled out. The aircraft dived straight through cloud and crashed onto cliffs just west of St Albans Head. In the same engagement Bann was credited with his second He 111, Hughes with a Do 17 and Me 110, Simmonds with a 110 and Wigglesworth with an unconfirmed 110. All of 238's pilots returned safely.

Bann was in action again later that afternoon (his fourth sortie of the day) when the squadron encountered a massive formation of 400 plus in the same area. A fast and furious dogfight followed, during which three German aircraft were confirmed destroyed with a further four damaged. Sgt Little, however, was shot down into the sea though he was picked up more or less unhurt. Bann was so exhausted that he apparently passed out in mid-air and when he came to he discovered that Marsh had vanished. He was never seen again. The ORB recorded his loss:

> Sgt Marsh was one of the early members of the Squadron and the leader of Yellow Section from the start. His quiet, painstaking personality made him popular and his section efficient.

Gordon Batt now became leader of the section. Despite their differences, he was greatly distressed by Marsh's death and stated that thereafter he made no more new friends as their loss was too painful.

At 4 p.m., as if by way of a parting shot, the aerodrome was attacked, with bombs falling behind 238's Dispersal, near to Wallop village. Drained and depleted, the squadron was only too glad to be going.

4
Old Crocks
(14 August–6 September 1940)

The following day the move to St Eval began, lock, stock and barrel, with 10 lorries for the baggage and 6 buses for the personnel. The Hurricanes were flown in by the available pilots, who included Bann, still grieving and guilt-stricken at the loss of Marsh. No. 604 Squadron had to loan them two pilots, including their CO, S/L Michael Anderson, who returned in the Blenheim that brought in 238's adjutant. On 15 August, the squadron received its first signal: 'WELL DONE 238 SQUADRON. A GREAT PART IN A GREAT DAY'. NEWALL.[48] The seventh letter was undated but probably written on the same day.

[Letter 7]

Sergeants' Mess,
RAF Station,
St Eval, Cornwall.
[15? August 1940]

Dear Mother and Father,

How's my good people at Macclesfield? I trust you are keeping well and in good spirit.

Well, here I am, an old crock so soon. I am afraid that our duty at the front line has told its tale upon our system. Our engagements have been really hectic and, unfortunately for us, we've always been there first, waiting for reinforcement, with the final result we are all down with nerve trouble and have been sent to this rest camp.

We have received a telegram from the Air Ministry congratulating us upon our very good work and wishing us good rest. But the cost has been heavy. Just Gordon Batt and I remain among the Sergeants and many of our Officers have gone. Just a very sad memory remains and worse for me, poor Tony Marsh, my section leader, and I were the last two in action and I think I must have done too much flying for I fainted and I, poor Tony's guard, left him to the mercy of all. Oh dear, I did feel bad when I learned he never came back.

This place brings back pleasant memories, for it was round here that my dear May and I spent our lovely holiday last year, Newquay, Carbis Bay, surf-riding and all that. We are getting out one day in three and I hope to visit some of these places. We are of course still flying, for it keeps us fresh and helps nerves, and have consequently flown over many places in Cornwall and Devon. Our new sector covers all Cornwall and most of Devon, but it's quiet and the 'Hun' does not come over in large numbers. Gosh, our last place, I began to dream of those hundreds we were always meeting.

What do you think of our efforts? Never did I think for one minute that we could hold back so large a number – planes just tumbled out of the sky. God but these grand lads are just giving their very all and some are very tired boys.

You will have to forgive me for not having written before this, but we have never left duty; our food and sleep have been obtained there.

How's Maurice getting along? I do hope he's getting settled. That, however, I don't think will cause Maurice much trouble. Please convey my kind regards to him. I will write to him if you will let me have his address.

How's Father getting along these days? I trust he's keeping well and getting just a little time off to enjoy this nice weather. We shall, I understand, be here for three weeks until we have become refitted and [taken on] new pilots, plus our troubles put right. I hope and wish that I could get May down for a short time. I don't think we shall get any time off or leave for we have proved good metal for the RAF and they require us back again.

Ah well, cheerio for now. All my kind regards,
                    Your loving Son
                           Eric

                             *

On 16 August, F/Lt Minden Blake took over as temporary CO. 'Mindy' Blake was twenty-seven and had been born in Ekatahuna, New Zealand. He was educated at Southland Boys' High School and Canterbury University College where he later became a Physics lecturer. His academic gifts were matched by his athletic prowess and he was a gymnastic champion and holder of the national pole-vaulting title. He had then volunteered for the RAF and received a commission in 1937. In 1940 he was instructing at Ternhill when he was posted to 238 Squadron to cover S/L Fenton's absence.

New Hurricanes also began to arrive and others were sent back for repair. The squadron was now covering large stretches of the West Country, but patrols were uneventful with 'nothing of note' becoming a standard entry in the ORB. Gordon Batt had time to visit Eric Seabourne in the naval hospital at Haslar and remembered sitting on his bed and asking him how he slept without eyelids. On the 17th the Secretary of State for Air, Sir Archibald Sinclair, was expected to visit but did not turn up, although a congratulatory signal was received from 10 Group.

Replacement pilots also started to appear. On 19 August, P/O Wladyslaw Rozycki and Sgt Frederick Sibley were posted from 6 OTU; next day P/O Richard ('Covey') Covington arrived from 226 Squadron. There was a notable loss, however, on the same day when F/O Howells, 238's

Engineer Officer, was transferred to the Headquarters of Fighter Command. The ORB lamented his departure:

> The squadron lost a Godfather rich in technical knowledge and beneficent in his labours to apply it. An officer of long service, having been a Halton boy, Sergeant Pilot, and a friend of Aircraftman Shaw,[49] he was well fitted by experience and a caustically kind nature, salted with Yorkshire wit, to nurse young pilots and bring the best out of his men.

No doubt he was given an appropriate send-off.

The relative tranquillity of St Eval was shattered at 2 p.m. on 21 August when a Ju 88 bombed and strafed the aerodrome. The adjutant of 238, in company with the adjutant of 236 Squadron, left the Officers' Mess 'in dignified haste' and were then spurred on their way when a bomb exploded nearby, blowing in parts of the glass corridor they were going along. They took shelter under the wall of the Officers' Cookhouse, not the best refuge as it was later noticed that the steam-heating system was centred there. From this vantage point they saw a Ju 88 release more bombs at an altitude of about 200 feet. The ORB takes up the story:

> [The bombs] fell and did not explode for an appreciable time; then the 236 hangar showed a pall of brown smoke with a centre of black and flame. The pilot was afraid of his job, as he pulled back his stick before letting go. The machine gunner began firing wildly, and the enemy shot up into the clouds with black boost tails from his engines. The damage done was the roof of the hangar disarranged and a Maggie [Miles Magister] completely wrecked...

Only three craters were found. The other bombs do not seem to have been traced.[50]

At 5 p.m. a patrol over the base engaged three Ju 88s and the one attacked by F/Lt Blake blew up in the air. Urwin-Mann chased another and shot it into the sea off Trevose Head. Wigglesworth discharged all of his ammunition into the third with little apparent effect.

John Urwin-Mann

That night a German aircraft dropped incendiaries in a line across the aerodrome without accomplishing any serious damage – 'but the scenic effect of burning grass and bracken was considerable. About an hour later another enemy aircraft dropped a shower of bombs which did not explode.' On 23 August, F/Lt Hughes undertook the squadron's first night operation, night flying practice having begun again a few days before. Later on there was another incendiary attack which once more looked more alarming than it was. The ORB noted drily: 'The flights put the fire out while the army remained ensconced in a trench.'

Bann's eighth letter refers to some of these events. Although it is dated '31 August 1940' in the Macclesfield booklet, a photocopy of the original shows it to have been undated. As Bann flew two sorties that weekend and was not therefore released from duty as the letter suggests, it is likely that the letter was written somewhat earlier.

[Letter 8]

Sergeants' Mess,
RAF Station,
St Eval,
Cornwall.
[*c.* 23 August 1940]

Dear Mother and Father,

Thank you very much for your letters. I am very sorry for not having written sooner, but dear old 'Jerry' has followed us down here and we have been quite busy knocking 'em down. All the people around here are very happy and at rest, for they have got to know that we are down here and our reputation has followed us, for all they say is 'Here come those fighter boys of the crack squadron'. Talk about free beer when we go into any of these Cornish taverns! My word, we feel very proud of these kind people's thoughts towards us.

Have received many letters and parcels from all of you and I am trying very hard to reply and offer my many thanks to all. Maurice, the Misses Slater, the Vicar, Mayor's Comforts Fund, all are very kind.

I am trying very hard to get Maurice posted down to my squadron. It would be fine for I could keep a Brother's eye upon him, plus help in any way, and we could go out together and I am very sure that Maurice would enjoy helping us in our squadron in its good work, seeing and helping his brother with the good work, so here's hoping.[51]

This good Cornish air has healed our war sores and very soon all of us hope to be again in action, driving back the invader. I understand that many in our squadron are soon to be recognised for their good work done.

A further pleasant surprise – May is coming down for a few days this coming weekend and to top the bill my Flight Commander has given me a few days' leave to enjoy myself along with my wife, so here's to a very pleasant weekend.

I read in the local Macclesfield paper that the seventeenth Spitfire will soon be given to the nation. 'Bravo, Macc!' All the boys of the RAF are amazed at this grand town. How I wish that I could be the lucky local boy to fly the plane.

Well, cheerio to you all,

Your loving Son,
Eric

In the final paragraph Bann was referring to popular campaigns such as 'Buy a Spitfire' that were sponsored by towns and cities eager to raise the funds to purchase one of Mitchell's planes for the nation. His home town was no exception and had recently received considerable local and national press coverage as a result of the magnificent gift of £100,000 by Mr Willard Garfield Weston, the Macclesfield MP, to replace fighter planes lost on 8 August. The town's latest fund was launched on 15 August, and it was decided that the name 'Macclesfield' and the town's coat-of-arms would be painted on the side of their plane. It was also hoped 'to get a Macclesfield pilot to fly the machine'. This obviously caught Bann's eye, for when he wrote to thank the Mayor's Comforts Fund for their latest gift, he again touched on the subject, mentioning that the RAF thought highly of Macclesfield because of the gift of sixteen fighters and adding 'now I understand you are well on the way to the seventeenth – what an encouragement for us boys.' He concluded: 'Having flown Spitfires quite a lot, I only wish that I could fly this Macclesfield Spitfire – a very proud fellow I should be.'[52]

By now night attacks with the preceding air-raid sirens were becoming so regular that pilots were getting too little sleep. It was decided to billet them out and the officers were accommodated at the Bedruthan Steps Hotel on the 26th, just in time to escape a heavy bombing raid that night on the aerodrome's false flight path. Sixty-two craters were reported, but the outcome was more agricultural than military in that an expanse of heather was cleared and a barren heath ploughed up for future crops. Next morning a Dornier 215, presumably sent to photograph the 'damage', was attacked by Blake and Considine and had to make a forced landing at Tavistock, its three crew members being made prisoners of war. The two pilots visited the scene to survey their handiwork and were photographed examining the propeller for the *Daily Mirror*. Later that day, while patrolling the base, Gordon Batt was miffed when he was shot at by the AA guns at Falmouth. On 28 August, the Sergeant Pilots (Bann, Batt, Domagala, Little, Pidd and Sibley) were billeted out at Douce Haft bungalow in Mawgan Porth. German bombers attacked the area the same night.

*

In early September Bann was granted ten days' leave and he and May travelled to Macclesfield to stay with his parents. They were joined by Maurice, who was given a special weekend leave to see him. Knowing that he would be in action again as soon as he returned, it was probably on this occasion that Bann asked his brother to look after May if he was killed.

A reporter from the *Macclesfield Times* also appears to have turned up, for an article entitled 'Wants to Fly the Town's Spitfire' was published on 12 September. It recorded Bann's high opinion of RAF bomber squadrons, of Polish airmen ('some of the finest') and of their German counterparts. He is described as being 'very modest about his achievements and experiences', though the writer credits him with the destruction of five German machines – a Dornier, two medium bombers and two fighters.[53]

Leslie Pidd also managed to snatch a brief leave around this time and returned to East Yorkshire for a belated birthday celebration with his family. He also finalised arrangements with his fiancée for their wedding, which was set for his next leave. On the following morning when he left to return to base, his young niece followed him to the bridge that crossed the dyke in front of their home. She called out to him and he came back to kiss her goodbye. She never saw him again.

In their absence several newcomers joined the squadron. On 31 August, P/O Robert Kings had arrived, followed on 2 September by two more Poles, Sgts Jozef Jeka and Stanislaw Duszynski. Jeka was six feet tall, blond and good looking. His main difficulty, according to Gordon Batt, was not repulsing the Germans but fending off the female of the species. Two more new faces appeared on the 7th, P/O James Tillet and Sgt Eric Guymer.

Meanwhile patrols continued, usually without incident, though on 1 September Batt and Domagala had chased a Ju

88 over Falmouth. It was noted that communication between the two pilots was difficult owing to the Pole's poor grasp of English and the plane had managed to escape. On the 3rd, Sgt Sibley crashed his Hurricane while landing and it had to be written off. The following day Batt was detailed to shoot down an escaped balloon, but it proved more elusive than the enemy. The 6th turned out to be 'a long day, trying to pilots in its ineffective results' as they endeavoured in vain to follow up reports of enemy action west of St Ives and on the Scillies. It was the lull before the storm.

Jozef Jeka

5
In the Thick of It
(10–29 September 1940)

The Blitz began on 7 September and the squadron's interlude at St Eval ended three days later when their Hurricanes and four troop carriers left for Middle Wallop. The following day they were back in action and the dreadful litany of casualties resumed. Just after 4 p.m., between Brooklands and Croydon, the twelve pilots of 'A' and 'B' Flights sighted 50 enemy bombers in a tight box formation with approximately 50 fighters 5,000 feet above. Owing to the haze the squadron became separated early in the engagement and a general mêlée ensued.

Batt saw an enemy plane plummeting past him and watched it all the way down as its wings fell off and the fuselage buried itself into the ground. 'That's saved someone from having to dig a grave,' he thought. His own squadron had mixed fortunes, however. Blake and Rozycki dispatched two of the bombers, but Towers-Perkins had to bale out and was taken to Tunbridge Wells hospital with serious burns and a leg wound. Worse still, Hughes and Duszynski were posted 'missing' and never seen again.[54] The ORB recorded their deaths:

> In F/Lt D. P. Hughes the squadron and the country has sustained a severe loss. Tall and fair, of a very quiet and sincere temperament, his performance showed him to be excellently suited to be a fighter leader. A son of the manse, he has proved yet again the sure foundation of a Puritan home. Long before his last flight he had earned the DFC, which it is hoped may yet be awarded.[55]

145

In Sgt Duszynski the squadron is robbed all too soon of the services of a Polish pilot. The sergeant had been in the squadron little more than a week and he had hardly any opportunity to maintain the valour and fortitude in aerial combat of his countrymen.

William Towers-Perkins

On 12 September, Davis and Simmonds engaged an enemy aircraft 4 miles east of Boscombe Downs and saw pieces coming off the top of the fuselage. The plane disappeared into clouds, having jettisoned its bombs, and no further trace of it was found. Later that day lorries and buses arrived from St Eval with the ground personnel and stores, thus completing the move. Four replacement pilots also arrived – P/O David Harrison, Sgt John McLaughlin and the first two Czechs to join the squadron, Sgts Vladimir Horsky and Jiri Kucera. Both had escaped from Czechoslovakia in 1938 and served with the French Air Force in the May–June period of 1940, during which

Kucera had destroyed three enemy aircraft. Next day S/L Fenton returned, refreshed but still carrying a scar on his forehead. On the 14th, Bann was back and reported some of the above events to his parents, including the news that the ever-dependable Domagala was out of action, though whether from injury or illness is not recorded.

[Letter 9]   Sergeants' Mess
                                                                      RAF,
                                                          Middle Wallop,
                                                                     Hants.
                                                    14 September 1940

Dear Mother and Father,

Letting you know that I have arrived safely.

Old 238 have been right in the thick of it – London every day. Good job I was far away for my leave; all the others recalled.

Domagala in hospital, also Towers-Perkins, May's pal. My Flight Commander, Mr Hughes, and one of the other Polish boys killed. Things have been rather warm.

Away for flying now. Was flying as soon as I landed.

Cheerio and thank you both,

Love
Eric

*

The tenth letter describes the events of Sunday 15 September 1940 – now celebrated as Battle of Britain Day – when the Germans launched two massive air attacks intended to break British resistance for good. The entire squadron was in action in the Brooklands–Kenley area, attacking in sections out of the sun. It had its most successful day ever, reflected in the following extracts from their combat reports:

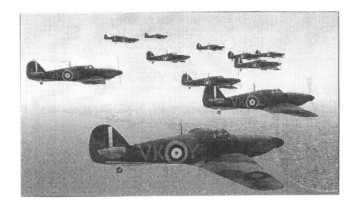

238 Squadron

I took the outside port E/A and fired 4-second burst from 150 yards from astern. The E/A drifted out of the formation and started to go down, port engine stopped. I broke away and saw 18 Do 17s flying North and turned to attack, but my windscreen was covered in black oil as a result of a bullet in oil pipe. I glided down after the He 111 and force-landed at West Malling alongside the E/A which had crashed on the aerodrome. 2 officers badly hurt but pilot uninjured and confirmed my statement.

(F/Lt Blake, Blue leader)

Squadron was at 24,000 and attacked in sections line astern. I attacked He 111 firing from starboard quarter burst of 3 seconds from 350 yards closing. The starboard engine caught fire and I continued attack from astern closing to approximately 25-50 yards firing all the time a burst of 5 seconds from astern. E/A made turn to right with engine on fire. I broke away to starboard and subsequently I saw E/A going down steeply emitting black smoke. Did not see crew bale out. On climbing up there was a series of explosions behind me and I saw a hole in the elevator and felt bullets against my armour plating, so having lost considerable height in evasive action considered it unwise to continue action and returned to base. Landed at Middle Wallop 1515. Number of rounds fired 1,600.

(P/O Simmonds, Red leader)

I fired a 2-second burst from 150 yards closing from full deflection at He 111 which burst into flames, turning to right and going right down out of control. Pilot believed shot. I followed E/A down and saw it hit ground. Went up and fired several short bursts of approximately one second at other E/A from 200 yards. Broke away and went below cloud where I saw single He 111 going South. I fired 2 short one-second bursts from 100 yards full quarter deflection. He lost height rapidly, one engine completely stopped and brown smoke coming out of port engine. Last burst penetrated front part of fuselage and my guns ceased as I had run out of ammunition. E/A was losing height rapidly, last seen at approximately 1,500 feet over sea and then turned towards land (off Eastbourne). Received return fire which was inaccurate.

(P/O Urwin-Mann, Green leader)

I fired short 1-second burst from under at 200 yards closing and broke away climbing. I then attacked an Me 110 from above full deflection firing 2-second burst at 200 yards closing and E/A started going down and then burst into flames. I followed him right down on to the ground where he hit and continued on fire. Two people jumped by parachute. I climbed up again and saw Hurricanes attacking Me 109 but could not catch it.

Went on to reserve and then had to force-land at East Grinstead in a field. Broke tail wheel and there was a hole in the starboard petrol tank. Landed at approximately 1530. Came on to Middle Wallop by train.

(P/O Covington, Green 3)

I fired at Me 110 for 2 seconds from 200 yards closing to 50 yards from underneath astern. At first the E/A dived in corkscrew and I followed and fired several 1-second bursts from astern. E/A went straight into ground after either pilot or rear gunner had baled out. I circled round and saw someone land by parachute and then climbed and attacked another E/A. I fired very short burst and then found all ammunition gone. The E/A had starboard engine smoking badly, belching smoke. Last seen heading South, chased by another Hurricane.

(Sgt Jeka, Yellow 3)

In all, eight pilots had accounted for 10 enemy aircraft: four He 111s and two Me 110s were destroyed; one He 111 was listed as a 'probable'; and two He 111s and one unidentified aircraft were damaged. However, four of 238's Hurricanes were beyond squadron repair and Leslie Pidd failed to return. Although the letter is dated '15 September 1940' in the Macclesfield booklet, it was written on the following day when Bann, who had been flying as Yellow 2, wrote to tell his parents of the titanic battle.

[Letter 10]

Sergeants' Mess,
RAF,
Middle Wallop,
Hants.

Monday.
[16 September 1940]

My Dear Mother and Father,

What about the RAF after yesterday! My gosh, for every bomb dropped upon the King and Queen[56] old 238 gave them hell. We got 12 'Huns' in one scrap. We just went in as one man and held our fire until very close range, then blew them right out of their cockpits. We're all just mad for revenge. Never again shall any one of us give any mercy, for our poor Flight Commander and yesterday the Yorkshire boy Sgt Pidd fell victim to these swines machine gunning whilst coming down by parachute. Now after seeing poor Pidd go, [we] shall never forgive the 'Hun'.

I am afraid that the weather will curb our activity, for it is raining hard. Still it will give rest to the over-worked, though mind you, we're for them now and we'll be quite content to fly any time.

Have felt much brighter after my visit home. Thank you all for the sincere kind actions shown to me. I really enjoyed myself and of course so did May.

Afraid that I can't find Maurice's address, so please enclose in your next letter.

Have found Mr Eseley's gift and will write and thank him in the next day or so.

Cheerio for now. All my kind regards to the people of Macclesfield.

Your loving Son
Eric

P.S. Domagala quite well. Will have to undergo an operation before fit for flying again. He's raising the place down – wants to be back among the Germans.

151

Uncertainty surrounds the death of Leslie Pidd to this day. The relevant ORB entry for 15 September records that 'one of our pilots (Sgt L. Pidd) was lost. Unfortunately, he was killed, his aircraft (P.2836) and his body being found some days later in a wood near Tonbridge... Of small stature, strong and closely knit, Sgt L. Pidd had been with the squadron since 18.7.40. He was the very best type of NCO pilot, and in him the squadron sustained another very serious loss.' The entry for 18 September notes that confirmation of his death had been received that day.

There are various versions of how he met his end. Bann's is one. Another is that he baled out when his aircraft was too low, while a third maintains that his parachute failed to open. What is known is that his fighter crashed into an oak tree in the grounds of Kent College School in Pembury, near to the main school building. In her book *The Kent College Saga*, Margaret James recalled the events of 15 September at the school:

> Term started in September as normally as possible, with further reduced numbers. It was then, at the time of the Battle of Britain, that the reality of war touched the school most closely when a British Hurricane fighter plane was shot down in the grounds by a German Messerschmitt. There are painful memories of the screaming noise as the plane descended. The inimitable Miss Barrett, Matron for many years at Folkestone and at Pembury, was first on the spot, and it was she who picked up the shattered remains of the dead pilot and covered the body in a cloth before the stretcher bearers arrived a little later. In 1975 a 'recovery' group from Brenzett Aeronautical Museum came with metal detectors and located pieces of the plane in the woods between Peter Pan and Wendy pools.

It seems from this account that Pidd did not bale out but came down with the plane and that his body was discovered immediately. Why it then took three days for confirmation to reach his base is yet another mystery. He was subsequently buried in the cemetery of St Peter's church in Woodmansey with full military honours and an RAF flypast.

The funeral procession of Sgt Leslie Pidd

*

For the next few days the squadron patrolled without incident as the Germans licked their wounds. On 18 September, it combined with 609 Squadron to form a wing for the first time. On the 21st, Bann was patrolling the base with Davis when the latter engaged a Ju 88 that was trying to bomb the aerodrome. Before coming to earth at Tangmere, the bomber was also attacked by Bofors gunfire and a Spitfire, but the victory was credited to Davis. Later that day their temporary CO, Minden Blake, left to take command of 234 Squadron at St Eval and 'the squadron lost a popular and charming cousin from New Zealand whose élan had served the squadron for far too short a time'.[57]

It was not only Bann who felt 'much brighter', for the whole squadron seemed to have been reinvigorated, as the ORB commented: 'About this time a great improvement was noted in the squadron's vitality – the glass doors of the mess having been in considerable jeopardy. A quick intensity of purpose rather than exuberance of spirits has so far been characteristic of this squadron. The improvement may be considered as the fruit of the change to St Eval.'

For a couple of days afterwards there was no operational flying owing to adverse weather conditions and Bann took the opportunity to write home. His eleventh letter has been provisionally dated from internal evidence – the references to London and the temporary lull in flying activities. He also mentions the death of John Allen who served with 54 Fighter Squadron. With Al Deere he had taken part in the celebrated Calais–Marck aerodrome rescue of the CO of 74 Squadron who had been stranded there. On 23 May 1940, they escorted a Miles Master to the airfield and then took on twelve Me 109s while the rescue was made. Allen was awarded the DFC on 11 June but was killed while making a forced-landing on 24 July. He was apparently known as 'the Bishop' because of his strong religious beliefs.

[Letter 11]   Middle Wallop,
                                                        Sunday.
                                          [22 September? 1940]

Dear Mother and Father,
    Thank you for your letter. Was very pleased to learn that all of you are keeping quite well.

154

We are still having plenty of fun down here, joining each day in the fun over London, plus a few visits around the camp.

Have enclosed the insurance receipt. Would you kindly let Mr Swaine have same when you next see him.

You will all be sorry to hear that the famous 'Bishop' John Allen has been killed in action. What a grand lad he was. Never shall I forget a very fine pal, ever cheery and always ready to do a good turn.

Have had a letter from Eric Heath. He enquires where Eric Swaine has got to these days, but I am afraid that I have lost touch myself. However, I must drop him a line.[58]

Not very many signs of any time off these days, not even 24 hours. We are not really flying a great deal but are ever on readiness for the unexpected.

Cheerio for now, all my kind regards,

Eric

*

Thereafter normal service resumed when the pace of battle quickened once more. On 25 September, the squadron intercepted 80 plus raiders on their way back from bombing Bristol and destroyed six He 111s and damaged two more. An extract from the combat report prepared for Fighter Command HQ evokes the determined ferocity of the attack:

> Blue 1 (P/O Urwin-Mann) fired two-second burst at He 111 from astern quarter at 200 yards closing right in. Bits flew off enemy aircraft but it did not break formation. Delivered similar attack firing 2-second burst from 150 yards closing to 70 yards. Received no return fire from enemy aircraft which then broke away and dived steeply. Followed and saw it turn on back out of control and fired another 2-second burst from 250 yards. Enemy aircraft

dived straight down and hit ground exploding. Made attack after regaining height on another He 111 and fired 2-second burst from 150 yards closing from quarter. One of the crew baled out and port engine blazing. Enemy aircraft dived steeply for coast line and Blue 1 followed firing 2-second burst from quarter at 150 yards to 100. Enemy aircraft turned shorewards and dived straight for house and burst into flames. Previously at 1,000 feet two more of crew baled out and landed in sea, being picked up by boats.

Blue 2 (P/O Rozycki) attacked He 111 from astern firing 2-second burst from 150 yards. Enemy aircraft left formation and Blue 2 delivered further attack from beam firing 2-second burst at 150 yards. Enemy aircraft turned on its back and dived to ground and burst into flames. Blue 2 saw crew bale out on parachutes.

All of 238's pilots eventually returned to base, some having landed at various points to refuel, others having lost their way. Sgt Sibley had to force-land near Bath and his aircraft was written off.

The following day their tally was even better, with seven aircraft downed and five damaged. This time, however, S/L Fenton made an emergency landing at Lee-on-Solent, while P/O Kings had to bale out with the whole of the bottom of his cockpit on fire. He landed safely and was soon back in the fray, but Sgt Horsky did not return. The ORB paid tribute through him to all of their foreign pilots:

Sgt Horsky was the first Czech pilot to be lost from this squadron; he had been with the squadron a fortnight and was the first Czech to join us. He had had but little time to get to know us, and, as in the case of his compatriots and of their Polish friends, diversity of language had set a hedge about him through which converse was not easy. It may be placed on record that the dash and bravery of these men is the more striking when it is remembered that they must pass many hours of loneliness in a strange country, even when surrounded with the pilots of their own squadron.

In the twelfth letter, written on this day, Bann acknowledges the help of the Polish pilot Jozef Jeka and mentions another of his friends from his time at Little Rissington, Sgt A. H. B. Friendship, who served with No. 3 Fighter Squadron. He had been commissioned in May 1940 when he also received his first DFM. A Bar followed that June. He would survive the war and leave the RAF in 1947 as a Squadron Leader. Bann ends with news of his own promotion prospects.

[Letter 12]

Sergeants' Mess,
RAF,
Middle Wallop,
Hants.
Thursday
26 September 1940

My Dear Mother and Father,

How's things Macclesfield way? Still enjoying the grand peaceful comfort? My word, the boys could not understand how I managed to find anywhere free from bombs. Things are really warm – never a night without a visit from Jerry and all day long we are knocking him away from London. Still, such is the day's work.

I wonder if you could forward to me my alarm clock in case. I am having great trouble in getting up these days, for we are going to bed and getting up at very odd times, just according to our friends' ebb and flow.

You'll perhaps be very pleased to learn that Domagala is getting along quite nicely, very anxious to be back with us again. His friend Jeka has been doing some very good work – my work has been relieved by the help of this very formidable pilot. Our squadron may well be called the International Squadron, for we have in our midst English, Scotch, Irish, New Zealanders, Australians, Polish, Czechs, Canadians. Not so bad – they are all a grand lot and good to know.

Have had a letter from May. She's very busy once again but feeling much better after the rest. Not a word was said from Jack or Mother upon our arrival, for I let them see that it was us doing the good turn coming back Thursday. A little bit of cheek now and again seems to pay.

How's Maurice? I wrote last time for his address so please let me have same, then I will write to him. I might even get over to see him if only I could get a few hours off.

Met one of the boys from Rissington yesterday. He tells me that my old pal Sgt Friendship has now the DFM and Bar and has also been made a Pilot Officer. Good boy, we had some grand times together. He's just over twenty years of age.

My report and recommendation for commission has now gone through. My word, my CO did give me a nice report and he added that I was strongly recommended for a Pilot Officer, so now I await the Air Ministry. I suppose they wonder what I am doing, first refused then accepted. Anyway, may it make or break me, I have decided to hold the first commission in our family.

Ah, well, cheerio for now. All my kind regards,

Your loving Son

Eric

*

On the afternoon of Saturday 28 September, Bann took off on his 60th sortie of the Battle of Britain, one of twelve pilots who encountered 25 Me 110s flying in a defensive circle east of the Isle of Wight. In what was to be the squadron's only success that day, Rozycki took one of them out: 'I dived from approximately 22,000 and fired [for] about 4 seconds from line astern about 200 yards. E/A very quickly turned and left circle and flew South, starboard engine in flames. I attacked again and fired rest of my ammunition at E/A... which then went down very slowly into the sea.' Rozycki returned to base just before the remainder of the squadron was surprised by 15 lurking Me 109s. Bann's plane was shot up by one of them as it flashed past him. 'Look out Gordon!' were his last urgent words. Batt peeled away and lost sight of his friend. Eye-witnesses saw Bann's plane on fire and heading towards Portsmouth. Seconds later he decided to bale out. His parachute did not open and he plunged to his death.

> To Maurice
> No 29
>
> From the leader of 238 Sqdn. 'Yellow Section' when his brother Eric, also a 'Sgt. Pilot RAFVR' was shot down behind me, with the warning
> "Look out Gordon"
> L.G. Batt.

Eric Bann's last words recorded by Gordon Batt in a presentation copy of his memoir to Maurice Bann

The following day May was officially informed that he had been killed:

Record Office,
Royal Air Force,
Ruislip,
Middlesex.
29 September 1940

Dear Madam,

It is my painful duty to confirm my telegram of to-day's date in which you were informed of the death of your husband No. 741589 Sergeant Eric Samuel Bann[59] of No. 238 Squadron, Royal Air Force, who was killed when the aircraft of which he was the sole pilot and occupant crashed in the vicinity of Bembridge at 3 p.m. on 28 September 1940 during an engagement with the enemy.

The Air Council desire me, in conveying this information to you, to express their sympathy and deep regret at your husband's death in his Country's service.

I am,
Dear Madam,
Your obedient servant,
(Signed) John Ramsey, W/Cdr

The ORB bade a final farewell to Eric Bann and to David Harrison and Ronald Little, both of whom were reported 'missing' in the same action. The body of the former was subsequently recovered on 9 October when it was washed up on Brighton beach; the latter was never found:

Sgt Bann, S. E., was one of the 'foundation' members of the squadron and was held in high esteem by all members of the squadron. He was an able and reliable pilot, and was very popular. He

160

took particular interest in the Polish pilots, doing them many little kindnesses and personal service.

P/O D. S. Harrison had been with the squadron only since 12 September. He was a VR who had graduated through the rank of Sgt. Pilot. His quiet, equable temperament gave promise of sound and useful performance to come, and his loss is greatly to be deplored.

Sgt. R. Little was also a 'foundation' member of this squadron. He was an able and reliable pilot who was highly esteemed by his fellow pilots.

This was a very bad day for the squadron.

6
'Lived Nobly, Died Nobly'
(30 September–31 October 1940)

'When Bann disappeared I was even worse,' wrote Gordon Batt. 'I didn't make friends at all.' He was the sole survivor of the original Yellow Section, but there was precious little time to grieve. On 30 September, he was back in the air on a patrol over Bournemouth when Robert Kings and Vernon Simmonds collided and had to bale out. Both landed safely, although Kings' parachute was ripped on the tail of his Hurricane as he left it and he was severely shaken after a heavy landing. This was the second time he had baled out in four days. In an engagement later that afternoon nine aircraft of the squadron took on 100 bandits twenty miles south of Portland, destroying four of them and damaging two more. Two accomplished pilots who had been transferred to the squadron on the day of Bann's death were involved. P/O Bob Doe, from 234 Squadron, was credited with an He 111, while F/Lt Michael Robinson, from 601, claimed two Me 110s destroyed and a probable Me 109. All the pilots returned to Middle Wallop where they refuelled and went on to Chilbolton, a satellite aerodrome in Hampshire and the new base for the squadron.

There the final month of the Battle of Britain began to play out. On 1 October, 'A' Flight joined 609 Squadron and intercepted an enemy raid heading south over Poole, which included bombers, fighters and two 4-engined Focke-Wulf Condors. Bob Doe was Red leader and made a vertical attack on the Condors. Covington shot down two 110s and damaged a 109 before his own Hurricane was destroyed by cannon fire. He escaped uninjured, but Sgt Sibley had disappeared, 238's last (and 17th) loss during the Battle. The ORB recorded: 'Of stocky build and solid character,

Sgt Sibley was lost before he had found the opportunity to show his mettle.'

'Covey' Covington

In his home town, the announcement of Bann's death was front page news. On Thursday, 3 October, the *Macclesfield Courier* reported:

> It is with intense regret that we learn of his death, and we sympathise greatly with his family; but they can find comfort in the knowledge that their son died defending his home and the women and children of his land from the threat from the air...
>
> So Sergeant Pilot Bann will not realise his cherished ambition and sit at the controls of the town's Spitfire. Nevertheless, he has set a glorious example of courage, gameness and determination.

The news devastated Bann's many friends, one of whom, Sergeant Alec Reid, wrote a letter of tribute to the local press on behalf of members of the Sergeants' Mess, 7th Battalion, the Cheshire Regiment. It read:

> It was with deep regret we learned of the death in action of Sergeant Pilot Eric Bann. Eric was very well-known and liked by members of our little Mess at the Drill Hall, Macclesfield, and it was a great shock to us when we received the news on Friday night.
>
> I have pinned on the wall in my billet a photo of a group of officers and NCOs of the RAF taken from a well-known weekly magazine after a success brilliantly executed and, standing at the back, with his usual happy face, is Eric. I have shown it to everyone who happened to visit me and have been proud to do so; I shall keep it now to remember him by.
>
> Eric was typical of what an Englishman should be – quiet and unassuming, always smiling and confident – a gentleman. God rest his soul.
>
> Our deepest sympathy is extended to his wife and family.
>
> 'We shall remember him.'[60]

On the 5th, his body was returned to Macclesfield and Inspector Butcher wrote to his mother concerning his possessions:

ISLE OF WIGHT CONSTABULARY
Sandown,
I.W.
5 October 1940

Dear Madam,

It is with the deepest regret that I am compelled to write to you in such circumstances as these, but I write with reference to personal property found on the late Pilot Sgt

Samuel Eric Bann of the Royal Air Force, Middle Wallop, home address 121, Bond Street, Macclesfield, Cheshire.

As you will have been previously informed, this gallant young man was shot down in aerial combat with the enemy over the Isle of Wight on Saturday, 28 September 1940, and it was most unfortunate that his parachute failed to function as it should have done, as we can ill afford to lose such men as these.

After communicating with his unit, I personally took charge of the arrangements made for the funeral as far as could possibly be done at this end and placed the matter in the hands of a local undertaker and, from personal experience, I am quite satisfied that everything will be to your satisfaction.

When I searched the body for the purpose of establishing his identity I found a number of things including a diary with snaps, etc., fountain pen, cigarette case, driving licence, wristwatch, crucifix, purse containing the sum of £2. 0s. 2d, and a registered letter containing a postal order for 20s, all of which I have in my possession and I shall be pleased to know to which address you would like this forwarded.

The three buttons I took from the airman's jacket as I thought perhaps some member of his family would like to have them.

The coffin was despatched to 121, Bond Street, Macclesfield, today by the 2.30 p.m. train from Portsmouth Harbour.

My heartfelt sympathy goes out to you and all the members of the family for it is such gallant men as this that are taking the brunt of the fight against a callous enemy, but their glorious exploits have earned for them the gratitude and admiration of the whole world and even the enemy knows what to do when he meets our wonderful Air Force which is comprised of such men as this. In fact their exploits are really astounding, but such are the qualities of the British airmen which can never be equalled.

In conclusion I would once again express my sympathy with you all and trust that you will give me instruction as to the property mentioned herein.

Thanking you,
I am Madam,
Yours faithfully,
W. Butcher
Inspector

The following month Bann's mother wrote to Inspector Butcher to see if she could elicit further details of her son's death and received the following reply:

ISLE OF WIGHT CONSTABULARY
Sandown,
I.W.
28 November 1940

Dear Madam,

I beg to acknowledge receipt of your letter of 26 November 1940 and, although you have given me something to think about, I will try to give you the facts as near as possible as I know them.

On the fatal day your son was engaged with other splendid fellows of the RAF in aerial combat with the enemy over this district and his machine later crashed.

I cannot give you any details as to what caused his machine to crash but can only assume that it was hit by enemy fire. While his fight was still in progress, the machine your son was piloting was seen flying at great speed towards Portsmouth, probably hoping to regain its base as I believe that it was on fire although not to any great extent.

When at a good height over Brading Marshes your son was seen to bale out quite safely but watchers who saw him come down say that his parachute did not open and this was found to be correct when Police and Military recovered his body shortly after. As regards the machine, this continued for a considerable distance out of control, pilotless, before finally crashing on the north side of Bembridge Downs about a mile away.

The machine was in little pieces strewn over about 200 yards of ground and I can only assume that the petrol tank exploded otherwise this would not have happened in the way it did.

As far as I could see your son was not wounded by the enemy as no gunshot wounds could be found on him at all but it was perfectly obvious that he died from a fractured skull as when he was examined by a doctor his skull was found to be badly fractured over the left eye caused through striking the ground.

There was no chance of life when found I am sorry to say. Had there been I would have worked hours as also would my men to have brought him round, but, under the circumstances, I could see that it was perfectly hopeless from the first.

One blessing is that your son did not suffer, for death according to the doctor was instantaneous.

I agree with you that at that time these gallant men must have been very much overworked but they have performed a most marvellous feat against overwhelming odds and have earned the gratitude of all the civilised world and such is the spirit of the British RAF that their names will live for ever as the saviours of our country of which we are all so proud.

Now madam I hope I have answered your letter to your satisfaction. I cannot tell you more with any degree of certainty.

I am most gratified to hear that you were so satisfied with my arrangements for the transferring of the coffin to Macclesfield, but I knew full well that the undertakers' work would be of the best.

I am sorry to say that I am now dealing with a similar crash which occurred here today under almost identical circumstances and I shall do my best for the relatives as I did in your case and, if the appreciation is as great, I shall think myself amply paid.

And now to offer my sincere sympathy once again,

I am Madam,
Yours faithfully,
W. Butcher
Inspector

*

As Bann's coffin was being transported to Macclesfield, 238 Squadron was again in action when twelve of its aircraft were bounced by fifteen marauding Me 109s north of Middle Wallop. None of its pilots was able to return fire and Sgt John McLaughlin had to bale out and was admitted to Shaftesbury hospital with multiple burns. Two days later, while intercepting about 100 raiders heading for Bristol, the squadron was again surprised by Me 109s diving out of the sun, and Covington took to his parachute for the second time in six days but suffered only minor injuries. Bob Doe accounted for a Ju 88 as did Urwin-Mann and Jeka, while S/L Fenton destroyed an Me 110. However, on the 10th, Doe's luck ran out when his Hurricane was critically damaged in an attack on 25 enemy aircraft flying in a very wide circle south of Warmwell. He 'hit the silk', covered in blood and unable to move his right foot or left arm. When he looked up at the canopy he saw that his parachute was torn and missing in places and he came down too quickly, landing on his bottom and then passing out. His Hurricane dived into the ground, narrowly missing the historic landmark of Corfe Castle.

Bob Doe (left)

Two days earlier, on Tuesday 8 October, no operational flying had taken place and a number of Bann's comrades-in-arms had travelled to Macclesfield for his funeral that afternoon. Part of the town came to a virtual stop, with large crowds lining the streets along which the cortege passed. The coffin was draped with the colours of the RAF and on top was his hat. Six sergeant pilots who were acting as bearers marched in front of the hearse, the top of which was covered with floral tributes. As it passed by, ex-servicemen stood to attention and women openly wept.

St Andrew's church was crammed to capacity so that many people had to stand in the porch, from where they joined in the prayers and the hymns 'Fight the Good Fight' and 'Abide with Me'. In a brief address, the Rev. P. D. Boulton said:

When we gather on an occasion like this, it is because of one who has loved the House of God... We are laying that one to rest. I can see here today a good many of the old associates of the late Sergeant Eric Bann, friends of his youth, a youth from which he had not grown. You come...because you held him in esteem, because you desire to pay last respects to one we know who lived nobly and died nobly. Perhaps no better words than those can be said...

I am very pleased that it has been possible to bring him to the church with which he was associated both as a child and as a man. We all feel sure that the character which he bore when he was among us was maintained when he was away from us, joining in that glorious band who are now doing the vital work of defending England against enemy air attacks. I am very pleased, too, to see that his comrades are represented here today as well as his friends... Our sympathy and prayers go out to those who feel their loss most.[61]

The route from the church to the Borough Cemetery was again lined with townspeople, and many more stood in silence among the graves in the windswept cemetery while the internment took place. As the coffin was lowered into the grave, the haunting notes of the Last Post were sounded by Leslie Riseley, one of the St Andrew's Scout Group.

Among the many scores of wreaths from family, friends and neighbours were several that reflected the various stages of Bann's short life. One was sent from the 20th Scout Group, another from the Sheet Metal Department of Fairey Aviation, a third from members of the congregation of St Andrew's church. Two were sent from his RAF comrades at Middle Wallop, the first from the CO and Officers, the second from the Warrant Officers, NCOs and airmen. His parents' card read: 'With all our love for our dear, brave and unselfish boy, from Mother, Father and Maurice. Not goodbye, but goodnight.' And from his young widow: 'To my dear husband, with love from May. God bless and keep you safe until we meet again.'

The grave of Eric Bann in Macclesfield cemetery

On Sunday 13 October, the monthly church parade of the St Andrew's Scout Group was dedicated to Sgt Bann. His widow meanwhile had presented the troop with the 'Eric Bann Trophy' in his memory, to be awarded for the monthly patrol competition. A few days later she received the following letter from Buckingham Palace:

171

The Queen and I offer you our heartfelt sympathy in your great sorrow. We pray that your country's gratitude for a life so nobly given in its service will bring you some measure of consolation. George R.I.

*

Operational flying for 238 Squadron began to wind down as enemy incursions decreased and the weather changed for the worse. Pilots came and went.[62] On 13 October, VHF was installed and was highly praised by everyone. Their HF radios had been prone to interference both from other sectors and also from the BBC Overseas Service, and 238 claimed to have gone into action on one occasion to the sound of 'A Nightingale sang in Berkeley Square'. Preparations for the further development of the aerodrome were also put in motion after a visit by Air Commodore Cole-Hamilton on the 15th, and the squadron made some changes of its own in the interim. On the 20th, the Officers' Mess was moved from beside the pilots' hut to a site a short way onto the Common. 'This move,' recorded the ORB, 'was a circus.' Boredom seemed to be setting in and the main risk came from accidents rather than enemy action. On 25 October, Wigglesworth indulged in a spot of low flying and hit the hedge between the pilots' hut and Orderly Room, breaking the Ops' phone line and scything off the top of the hedge. Remarkably he landed safely, whereupon he was placed under open arrest pending a court martial. (He was later found guilty and fined.)

The Battle of Britain ended for the squadron on an anticlimactic note. On 31 October, a dull thick day, no sorties were flown and then the rain began, 'gathering and flooding down off the landing ground. It flowed through the hedge in a torrent several inches deep. The officers'

172

Mess tent was nearly blown away and the men's Mess tent went down.'[63]

The recognition that Bann foresaw began to be made with DFCs awarded to Bob Doe and Charles Davis in October. More were to follow, though there would be no posthumous award for Bann, however richly deserved.

7
Ad Finem: To the End
(Afterword)

In May 1941, the Squadron was sent to the Middle East and was in action throughout the desert campaign in support of the 8th Army. It was then withdrawn to Egypt and converted to Spitfires. In March 1944, the squadron was posted to Corsica for sweeps over northern Italy and later provided air cover for the Allied landings in southern France. After withdrawing to Naples, the squadron was eventually disbanded on 31 October 1944.

238 Squadron in the Middle East

The final (handwritten) entry in the ORB paid a last tribute to all those who had served since May 1940:

> The Squadron has been disbanded but its reputation as one of the finest Fighter Squadrons of the war will live for ever in the annals of the Royal Air Force. The fine spirit of comradeship and co-

174

operation which existed amongst Officers and Men since the Squadron's reformation has been an inspiration to all who came into contact with us and was one of the main contributions to the successes obtained...The letters 'K.C.'[64] may not be seen again but the spirit of the Squadron motto *'AD FINEM'* will remain with the old members wherever they may be.

*

John Anderson ('Andy'), the sole survivor of the trio, re-joined 253 Squadron and was shot down on 14 September 1940, suffering serious injuries and becoming another member of the Guinea Pig Club. He eventually returned to non-operational flying duties and at the end of the war left the RAF as a Flight Lieutenant, whereupon he worked for an agricultural supplier. He died in 1978, aged 61.

Gordon Batt served with the squadron in Egypt and then in 1942 returned to the UK to act as an instructor. He ended the war as a Flight Lieutenant and re-joined Daimler in Coventry. He died in 2004.

Minden Blake was awarded the DFC in 1940 and the DSO in 1942. He was shot down during the Dieppe raid and spent the rest of the war as a POW at Stalag Luft 111. He retired from the RAF in 1958 with the rank of Wing Commander and died in 1981.

Brian Considine was shot down over Bournemouth on 5 November 1940 but soon recovered and returned to the squadron. He went on to serve in the Middle and Far East and was released from the RAF in 1945, whereupon he flew for Aer Lingus for several years. He died in 1996. He is one of eight Battle of Britain pilots (all former pupils) commemorated on a plaque at Ampleforth College.

Richard Covington moved to 303 Squadron in December 1940, but a few weeks later he was interned in the Irish Republic after a ferry plane he was on had to force-land there. He was liberated in 1944 when internment ended and then flew with 127 Squadron from various airfields on the continent. He retired from the RAF in 1964 as a Flight Lieutenant. He died in 1994, aged 73.

Charles Davis was killed in 1941 when he flew into a hill in thick cloud. He was 20.

Bob Doe re-joined 234 Squadron in December 1940 and the following month was seriously injured when he crash-landed at night. He later served as an instructor before commanding 613 Squadron during the Burma campaign. He retired from the RAF in 1966 as a Wing Commander and then ran a garage in Rusthall, Kent. He died in 2010. With 14 victories and two shared, he was one of the outstanding aces of the Battle of Britain.

Marian Domagala went on to serve with several other squadrons before becoming an instructor, and was awarded the Polish Cross of Valour with two Bars. He left the RAF in 1946 as a Flight Lieutenant and settled in Scotland. He died there in 1991.

'Jimmy' Fenton held several high appointments in the Middle East where he was given command of 243 Wing and then of 212 Group. In 1943 he returned to the UK to take command of the Kenley fighter sector and went on to play a leading role in the preparations for D-Day. He was awarded the DFC (1942), the DSO (1943) and mentioned in despatches three times. He was released from the RAF in 1945 as a Group Captain and made a CBE in 1946. From 1949 to 1952 he was General Manager of BOAC and later Managing Director of the Peter Jones' store chain. He retired in 1958 and moved to Jersey where he died in 1995, aged 86.

Eric Guymer served with 238 Squadron until 1941. He left the RAF in 1945 as a Flight Lieutenant.

Jozef Jeka went on to serve with various squadrons and was in action for most of the war except for a spell as an instructor. He was awarded the DFM (1942), the *Virtuti Militari* (Poland's highest decoration for heroism), the Cross of Valour with three Bars and the Silver Cross of Merit. He finally commanded 306 Squadron and left the RAF in 1947 as a Flight Lieutenant. It is reported that he was killed in a plane crash in Indonesia in 1958 while flying a clandestine mission for the CIA.

Robert Kings went on to serve in the Middle East and India before returning to the UK in 1947. He retired from the RAF in 1964 as a Flight Lieutenant.

Jiri Kucera received the French *Croix de Guerre* with three palms and two stars and the Czechoslovak *Croix de Guerre* for his service in France. He was commissioned in 1941 and after the war returned to Czechoslovakia. He died in 1980.

James McArthur went on to have considerable success with 609 Squadron before suffering damage to his hearing and losing his operational category. He received the DFC in 1940 and left the RAF in 1947 as a Wing Commander. He died in a flying accident in America in 1961.

John McLaughlin became another of McIndoe's Guinea Pigs when he was sent to the Queen Victoria Hospital, East Grinstead, for treatment for his burns. He was commissioned in 1943, and on his release from the RAF in 1946 as a Flight Lieutenant he emigrated to Australia. He died in 2001.

Michael Robinson left 238 to take command of 609 Squadron on 5 October 1940 and was awarded the DFC the following month and the DSO in August 1941. With a significant number of 'kills' to his credit, he was posted to lead first the Biggin Hill Wing and then the Tangmere Wing. In 1942, whilst leading the Wing, he vanished without trace. He is remembered on the Runnymede Memorial.

Wladyslaw Rozycki served with several other squadrons and received the DFC (1942) and many Polish decorations. He was demobilised in 1946 and two years later emigrated to Canada where he died in 1970.

Eric Seabourne spent seven months undergoing plastic surgery before returning to service. He was commissioned in 1941 and awarded the DFC a year later. He had attained the rank of Squadron Leader by the time of his retirement from the RAF in 1960.

Vernon Simmonds went on to serve with 118 Squadron and then 333 Squadron and also spent time as a Chief Gunnery Instructor. He left the RAF in 1946 as a Squadron Leader and died in 2005.

James Tillet was shot down and killed in November 1940.

William Towers-Perkins was at the East Grinstead hospital on and off for 18 months. He became another founder member of the Guinea Pig Club and its first honorary secretary. After he was released from the RAF in 1946, he joined Air Traffic Control and remained in Civil Aviation. He died in 2001, aged 82.

John Urwin-Mann was awarded the DFC in November 1940 for displaying 'initiative and dash in his many engagements against the enemy' during which he destroyed at least eight enemy aircraft. He then saw further action with 238 in the Middle East before being given command of 80 Squadron in 1942. In the same year he gained a Bar to his DFC and, after leading 126 Squadron on operations from Malta in 1943, he was awarded the DSO. He retired from the RAF in 1959 as a Squadron Leader and, after a variety of selling posts, worked for NatWest Bank until his retirement. He died in 1999.

After his low-flying escapade, John Wigglesworth was transferred to 67 Squadron in December 1940 and served with it in the Far East. He was killed in 1942 whilst making a forced landing and is buried in Rangoon War Cemetery in Burma. He was 21.

*

After the war, George Pidd worked as a traffic warden at Dunswell School where his late son Leslie had been a pupil. Whenever 11 November fell during the school week, he would enter the senior classroom, come to attention before a photograph of his son that hung from the wall near the headmistress's desk and salute it. He would then walk out without saying a word.

Sgt Leslie Pidd

*

In 2010 Vicky Vizard, a thirteen-year-old pupil at Kent College, began researching the life of Sgt Leslie Pidd whose Hurricane had crashed near the school on 15 September 1940. Her interest had been sparked by her father, Stephen, the founder and Managing Director of Airframe Assemblies, a company that rebuilds Spitfires and Hurricanes and other planes, who had spoken about the crash site to his daughter.

Her research culminated in the installation of a commemorative plaque at the school and an unveiling ceremony on 15 September 2010 at the precise moment that the Hurricane came down. More than thirty of Sgt Pidd's relatives attended, some meeting one another for the first time. Nic Morton, the great nephew of the pilot, arrived on the 14th to witness further excavation of the crash site:

> A number of fragments had already been uncovered and were laid out on a folded white bulk bag. The finds included fragments of Perspex, a small section of the instrument panel, an engine valve and spring, a battery lead, fragments of tyre, a tyre valve, a small brass plate with an inscription indicating the fluid level and a large number of engine casing fragments. One of these, when the soil was scraped away, revealed the smell of engine oil still preserved after seventy years.

The next day he attended the Senior School assembly which included a presentation on the pilot. Afterwards there were several radio and TV interviews before other relatives and guests began to arrive. The following paragraphs are extracts from Nic's account of the service of commemoration that took place later that afternoon:

MEMORIAL SERVICE FOR SERGEANT LESLIE PIDD

Before long Steve and Andrea Vizard arrived with the historian and TV presenter Jules Hudson, so it was handshakes and warm greetings all around. The first family to arrive was Marjorie, Leslie's niece, along with her niece and three grandchildren. Marjorie reminded me of my Grandma and we had a hug, having met for the first time ever. This was to be the first of many first meetings for me that day. When Marjorie saw the Memorial Mosaic she cried.

Across the car park I could see my sister and her family and Mum and Dad along with Jill Pidd, another of Leslie's nieces, whom I recognised from nearly forty years ago. She showed me a letter that she had received the previous day. After the war Leslie's fiancée had married and had recently died. Her daughter, who was aware of the Memorial, wanted Jill to have her Mum's pendant, which had a faded colour photograph of Leslie in it and a cross on the same chain. It was very touching and something that had made Jill cry with emotion. I asked her if she would read the letter during the service and she readily agreed.

I had been introduced to Harry Matthews, the Chaplain, during the morning and we had spoken of how things would work out in practice. It was now time to assemble. The schoolgirls sat in rows on the grass and the family and guests arranged themselves in a line facing the school. The staff were arranged around the outside and facing the same way as the pupils. A lectern was provided at the right-hand corner and a P.A. system set up with a microphone for the speakers. On the left was the chamber choir. Over the lunchtime period the weather had dulled slightly, but as the service began the sun came out strongly to help illuminate us all.

After a short introduction by the Headmistress, Sally-Anne Huang, we sang the first hymn 'Lord for the Years'. The singing, despite our being outside, was better than the morning's effort, boosted by the choir. Then Jules Hudson took the stand and gave a fitting and well-polished account of Leslie's service with the RAF and his role in the Battle of Britain. Jules was not a celebrity seeking media exposure but a person who had taken a real interest in Leslie's story and the unusual events that had connected so many people and were down to a year 9 pupil, Vicky Vizard.

The family and guests were then led down to the memorial by Harry Matthews for the dedication of the mosaic with prayers and quiet reflection. On our return to the main area, Jules Hudson recited Magee's poem 'High Flight' after explaining the circumstances of its writing.

Memorial Mosaic

I then gave my short talk and 'thank you's' on behalf of the family. Afterwards Jill came forward to tell the assembled group about the pendant she had received. Marjorie then took over and told everyone the story of her last contact with her Uncle Leslie. He had been home from leave and the following morning he left to return to base, but Marjorie followed him to the little bridge that crossed the dyke in front of their home. She called for Leslie and he came back to say goodbye and give her a kiss. A few days later he was killed in action. She had been the last family member to see him alive. It was very moving to hear.

The school song was sung next which included a line that now took on true significance – 'Where many died for freedom in our Kentish fields and skies' – and then Harry Matthews led us in prayers. As he did so, the choir sang a chorus and the whole thing brought me close to tears. After this, the choir sang 'The White Cliffs of Dover' in the most beautiful voices you could imagine. Before too many verses had been sung the sound of the Merlin took over and the handsome, honest Hurricane flew up the valley alongside the school. A cheer could be heard from the Prep School children who were outside and right under the flight path of the wonderful fighter. The tribute finished with a victory roll over the site of the crash and then silence as it faded from sight. The choir sang 'The White Cliffs' again for everyone and as they finished we witnessed the beautiful sight of the Spitfire and the ensuing air display to pay tribute to Sergeant Pilot Leslie Pidd.

Now that the formal part of the day had ended people stood and chatted, many of us knowing that it would be some time, if ever, that we might meet again. There were lots of hugs and warm handshakes between relative strangers and only permitted in such poignant circumstances. Caring embraces between family members too. One teacher remarked that they had stood in tears during the service. Andrea Vizard said that it was the most moving memorial service she had ever attended.

Anthony, who worked at the school, volunteered to organise the time capsule that had been suggested the previous day. He would get a suitable bottle and insert a copy of the Memorial Day programme before refilling the crash site crater with earth. Just in case future generations decide to excavate again.

We all drove away overwhelmed by the event and we will be for ever grateful to everyone who made the Memorial Day possible.

Insignia of 238 Squadron

NOTES

1. Now renamed All Saints.
2. *Macclesfield Courier*, 3 October 1940. Edgar James Kain, a New Zealander nicknamed 'Cobber', was the first RAF ace of the war. He was killed in a flying accident in June 1940.
3. *Macclesfield Courier*, 11 January 1940.
4. *Ibid.*, 1 February 1940.
5. Letter to the author, 26 October 2005.
6. Letter to the author, 17 October 2005.
7. Letter to the author, 4 October 2005.
8. L.G. Batt, *Sgt Pilot 741474 RAFVR*, p.21.
9. S/L Eric Douglas Elliott who was captured and became a prisoner of war.
10. Both flight commanders, Guy Harris and Harry Anderson, were lost on 19 May. Harris was wounded but survived; Anderson was killed.
11. The first intake consisted of P/O J. S. Wigglesworth, F/O C. Howells (Engineer Officer) and Sgt E. R. Alsop (12 May); P/O C. T. Davis, P/O B. Firminger and F/O D. C. MacCaw (13 May); P/O B. B. Considine and Sgt H. J. Marsh (14 May); and P/O J. R. Urwin-Mann, F/Lt S. C. Walch, F/Lt J. C. Kennedy and Sgt C. Parkinson (15 May). Later that month more 'foundation' members arrived: Sgt Bann and Sgt Batt (21 May); Sgt J. Gardiner and Sgt R. Little (24 May); and F/O A.N. David (25 May) who was to serve as Adjutant.
12. Marsh diary.
13. *Ibid.*
14. *Ibid.*
15. Email to the author, 30 September 2013. Reference books often give Urwin-Mann's nationality as British.

[16] Marsh diary. The ORB records that Urwin-Mann arrived on the 15th , so he must have stopped off elsewhere.

[17] Marsh diary.

[18] *Ibid.*

[19] *Ibid.*

[20] *Ibid.*

[21] Sgt Alsop was posted away from the squadron on 17 July 1940, Sgt Gardiner on 14 September 1940. Neither took part in the Battle of Britain.

[22] Fairey Aviation Company.

[23] Eric's cousin who was a Sgt Observer with 53 Squadron. He was reported missing on 28 August 1940, aged 22, and is remembered on the Runnymede Memorial.

[24] Letter to the author, 29 October 2005.

[25] Quoted in the *Macclesfield Times*, 29 August 1940.

[26] ORB.

[27] *Ibid.*

[28] Marsh diary.

[29] *Ibid.*

[30] *Ibid.*

[31] *Macclesfield Courier*, 18 July 1940.

[32] Maurice Bann wrote to the author: 'Gordon had acquired an MG (TA Midget) 1936 approx. and he and Eric used to travel up to Birmingham whenever possible. Eric's wife lived in Birmingham.'

[33] Marsh diary.

[34] Fenton, *Aquarius,* p.46.

[35] 501 Squadron lost 19 pilots. Harold Fenton in his memoir *Aquarius* states that his squadron had 18 pilots killed in the Battle of Britain but would seem to be including Brian Firminger who died just before the battle started.

[36] Batt, *op.cit.*, pp.34-36.

37 Marsh diary.

38 'Overboost', a form of emergency power.

39 A handwritten note in the ORB states that he died before reaching land; other accounts report that he died the following day.

40 Marsh diary.

41 *Ibid.*

42 There is one discrepancy concerning this aircraft that was presumably lost in the Channel. On the sortie of 27 July, the ORB gives P.2947 as the number of Sgt Bann's Hurricane and P.3823 as S/L Fenton's. However, according to the ORB, P.2947 was still being flown on 1 August (by Sgt Seabourne) and on 2nd (by P/O Simmonds). On 8 August P.3823 is listed as the Hurricane being flown by F/Lt Turner when he was lost over the Channel; confusingly, it is also given as the number of the plane flown by S/L Fenton who set off in a vain search for Turner and who had to ditch into the Channel that day. Other reference works now state that Fenton was flying P.2947. If this was the case, and if 27 July was the date of the above episode, the only conclusion to be drawn is that Bann was flying a different Hurricane from the one specified in the ORB.

43 His mother's birthday was 3 August.

44 This is inexplicable and denied by evidence in the letter. Should it perhaps read 'for three hours'?

45 Fenton, *op.cit*, p.52.

46 *Macclesfield Times*, 29 August 1940.

47 He had joined on 7 July.

48 Air Chief Marshal Sir Cyril Newall, Chief of the Air Staff.

49 The name under which T. E. Lawrence (of Arabia) served in the RAF.

[50] One was discovered in a field by workmen laying new water mains in 2013 and detonated by a bomb disposal unit.

[51] Maurice was an aircraftman and had been stationed at RAF Melksham (No 12 School of Technical Training). He later worked as ground crew on Lancasters.

[52] *Macclesfield Times*, 12 September 1940.

[53] This information presumably came from Bann. Latter-day reference books credit him with half this number, though none mention the possible kill of 7 July 1940, for which the letter is the only evidence. Christopher Shores (*Those Other Eagles*, p. 36) gives his tally as 2 confirmed (the Me 110 on 13 July and the He 111 on 13 August), 2 shared destroyed (the He 111 on 11 August and a Ju 88 on 21 September) and one shared unconfirmed (a Do 17 on 13 July). Eric was indeed present when the Ju 88 and Do 17 referred to were brought down, but contemporary records suggest that he did not participate in the action. As only two of his combat reports survive, it is now impossible to establish an exact figure.

[54] Duszynski's Hurricane was discovered and excavated in 1973 but no body was found.

[55] His DFC was awarded in 1941 with effect from 21 August 1940.

[56] A reference to the bombing of Buckingham Palace.

[57] ORB.

[58] Eric Swaine had also joined the RAFVR and served with 21 Bomber Squadron. He was awarded the DFC in 1944 when he was a Flight Lieutenant. He survived the war and became Honorary President of the Macclesfield Historical Aviation Society.

[59] In RAF records (except 238's ORB) his forenames are given in this order. However, since Eric signed himself 'S. E. Bann' and as this is how his name appears in

Macclesfield newspapers and on his gravestone, it is the preferred order elsewhere.

[60] *Macclesfield Courier*, 10 October 1940.

[61] *Macclesfield Times*, 10 October 1940.

[62] Newcomers during this period included P/O B. G. Collyns (30 September); P/O R. W. Clarke and P/O P. J. Morgan (5 October); P/O R. B. Rohacek, P/O A. McInnes and Sgt F. A. Bernard (8 October); F/Lt W. G. Measures (12 October); and F/Lt J. A. O'Neill, DFC (21 October).

[63] ORB.

[64] The latest squadron code.

Select Bibliography

Max Arthur, *Forgotten Voices of the Second World War* (London, 2004)

Max Arthur, *Last of the Few* (London, 2010)

William Ash, *Under the Wire* (London, 2005)

Roy Asser, *The Battle of Britain: the Camera's View* (privately printed, 2006)

L. G. Batt, *Sgt Pilot 741474 RAFVR, A Flying Memoir 1938-1959* (privately printed)

Battle of Britain Memorial Flight Yearbook 2012

Patrick Bishop, *Fighter Boys* (London, 2003)

Patrick Bishop, *The Battle of Britain* (London, 2009)

Martin W. Bowman, *Scramble* (Gloucestershire, 2006)

Chaz Bowyer, *Fighter Pilots of the RAF 1939-1945* (South Yorkshire, 2001)

Alan Brown, *Airmen in Exile* (Stroud, 2000)

Peter Brown, *Honour Restored* (Kent, 2005)

Stephen Bungay, *The Most Dangerous Enemy* (London, 2000)

Richard Townsend Bickers, *The Battle of Britain* (London, 1990)

Adam Claasen, *Dogfight* (South Yorkshire, 2013)

Tim Clayton & Phil Craig, *Finest Hour* (London, 2001)

Richard Collier, *Eagle Day* (London, 2001)

Brian Cull & Bruce Lander, *Twelve Days in May* (London, 1995)

Brian Cull & Roland Symons, *One-Armed Mac* (London, 2003)

Steve Darlow, *Five of the Few* (London, 2006)

Martin Davidson & James Taylor, *Spitfire Ace* (London, 2004)

Alan Deere, *Nine Lives* (Kent, 1991)

Len Deighton, *Battle of Britain* (London, 1981)

Bob Doe, *Fighter Pilot* (Kent, 2006)

W. G. G. Duncan-Smith, *Spitfire into Battle* (London, 1981)

H. A. Fenton, *Aquarius, A Flying Memoir 1928-1945* (privately printed)

Norman Franks, *Air Battle Dunkirk* (London, 2000)

Sebastian Faulks, *The Fatal Englishman* (London, 1997)

Guy Gibson, *Enemy Coast Ahead* (1944)

Jonathan Glancey, *Spitfire, the Biography* (London, 2006)

Richard Hillary, *The Last Enemy* (London, 1942)

Tony Holmes, *Hurricane Aces 1939-40* (Oxford, 1998)

David Irving, *Göring* (London, 1989)

Margaret James, *The Kent College Saga* (Governors of Kent College, 1986).

'Johnnie' Johnson, *Wing Leader* (London, 1990)

Philip Kamplan & Richard Collier, *The Few* (London, 1990)

Michael Korda, *With Wings Like Eagles* (London, 2009)

Jon Lake, *Battle of Britain* (Northants, 2000)

Barry M. Marsden, *Portraits of Heroes, Derbyshire Fighter Pilots in the Second World War* (Gloucestershire, 2011)

David Masters, *So Few* (London, 1946)

Geoff Mayer and Chris Sheldon, *The Wolstanton Roll of Honour* (2012)

E. R. Mayhew, *The Reconstruction of Warriors* (London, 2004)

Gordon Mitchell, *R. J. Mitchell, From Schooldays to Spitfire* (Buckinghamshire, 1980)

Bob Ogley, *Biggin on the Bump* (Westerham, 1990)

Matthew Parker, *The Battle of Britain* (London, 2000)

Alfred Price, *The Battle of Britain: The Hardest Day* (London, 1979)

Jeffrey Quill, *Spitfire: A Test Pilot's Story* (Manchester, 1998)

Winston G. Ramsey (ed), *The Battle of Britain, Then and Now* (London, 1980)

Anthony Robinson, *RAF Fighter Squadrons in the Battle of Britain* (London, 1991)

Derek Robinson, *Invasion 1940* (London, 2005)

Dilip Sarkar, *How the Spitfire Won the Battle of Britain* (Gloucestershire, 2013)

Andy Saunders, *Convoy Peewit* (London, 2010)

Ted 'Shippy' Shipman, *One of the Few* (Barnsley, 2008)

Christopher Shores, *Those Other Eagles* (London, 2004)

Christopher Shores & Clive Williams, *Aces High* (London, 1994)

Richard C. Smith, *Hornchurch Eagles* (London, 2002)

Edward Smithies, *Aces, Erks and Backroom Boys* (London, 2002)

Peter & Dan Snow, *Battlefield Britain* (London, 2004)

Tommy Steele, *Bermondsey Boy* (London, 2006)

Nick Thomas, *Ben Bennions, DFC* (South Yorkshire, 2011)

Nick Thomas, *Kenneth 'Hawkeye' Lee, DFC* (South Yorkshire, 2011)

Nick Thomas, *Stafford at War 1939-1945* (South Yorkshire, 2009)

Graham Wallace, *RAF Biggin Hill* (London, 1959)

R. W. Wallens, *Flying made my Arms Ache* (privately printed, 1990)

Geoffrey Wellum, *First Light* (London, 2003)

Kenneth G. Wynn, *Men of the Battle of Britain* (Norfolk, 1989)

Newspapers/booklets:
Evening Sentinel
Macclesfield Courier
Macclesfield Times

Quotations from the letters of Eric Bann and the war memoir of Dennis Armitage are from *Eric* (1988) and *Squadron Leader Dennis L. Armitage, DFC* (1989), two booklets issued by the Macclesfield Historical Aviation Society.

Unpublished material:
The National Archives: the Operations Record Books of 253 and 238 Squadrons (Air 27/1511 and Air 27/1453) and combat reports of 238 Squadron (Air 50/91)

The Imperial War Museum: MS Diary of H. J. Marsh (Doc. 12822) and recorded interviews with Brian Bertram Considine (Cat. No. 10961), Leslie Gordon Batt (Cat. Nos. 21873 and 28573) and Eric William Seabourne (Cat. No. TV 129X)

Stoke-on-Trent City Archives: Tape recording (T243) of John Ashton talking about flying the Hurricane and Spitfire

Index

By the same author:

Wings Over Meir: the Story of the Potteries Aerodrome
(Amberley, 2010)

Wings Over Meir is a highly readable and meticulously researched account of the Potteries' now largely forgotten aerodrome. In setting the scene, the author traces the district's long history of involvement in aerial pursuits, from balloon ascents and death-defying parachute drops to some of the country's earliest flying and gliding exhibitions. Among a host of memorable characters are Dolly Shepherd, Samuel Cody, Gustav Hamel, Harold Hales and Reginald Mitchell - a young witness to some of these thrilling (and at times hilarious) events.

After the development of the aerodrome, flying activities were concentrated at Meir and the airfield welcomed some of the most celebrated airmen of the day, including Charles Barnard, Sir Alan Cobham and Charles Scott. Their hugely popular 'flying circuses' are vividly evoked within these pages.

It was, though, as an RAF training school that the aerodrome came into its own, first as a base for the fledgling pilots of the Volunteer Reserve, then as a full-time RAF station upon the outbreak of war. The book profiles some of the pilots who trained there, including at least twelve of 'The Few', one of the Dam Busters, and four of those who took part in The Great Escape from Stalag Luft III. This fascinating glimpse into the area's heroic past is also a moving tribute to those who did not return.

Now available on Kindle.

Theatres of War deals with three highly significant moments in the history of the Midlands. In 1891 the visit to Stoke of William Cody ('Buffalo Bill') created a sensation, for he was one of the most famous and charismatic figures of his age. It was the beginning of a notable association with the area, for Cody not only performed in the Potteries on three separate occasions but also rehearsed and established his winter quarters there. His Wild West, one of the most spectacular shows ever seen, was truly a theatre of war, vividly recreating such events as Custer's last stand at the Little Bighorn.

The Minnie Pit explosion of 1918 was the worst disaster in the history of coal mining in North Staffordshire in which 156 men and boys were killed. The tragedy moved the whole nation and inspired Wilfred Owen to write his poem 'Miners' in which the devastation at Halmerend became a metaphor for the carnage he had witnessed on the Western Front.

The assassination of SS General Reinhard Heydrich in 1942 provoked a terrible act of reprisal – the destruction of the Czech mining village of Lidice. In response, the defiant *Lidice Shall Live* campaign that originated in Stoke-on-Trent became a worldwide movement to confront and confound Nazi brutality.

Forthcoming in 2015 from the North Staffordshire Press.